The Handbook of Law Firm Mismanagement for the 21st Century

Other Books by Arnold B. Kanter

The Essential Book of Interviewing
The Lawyer's Big Book of Fun
Was That a Tax Lawyer Who Just Flew Over?
The Ins & Outs of Law Firm Mismanagement
Advanced Law Firm Mismanagement
The Handbook of Law Firm Mismanagement
The Secret Memoranda of Stanley J. Fairweather

The Handbook of Law Firm Mismanagement

for the 21st Century

by Arnold B. Kanter

illustrated by Paul Hoffman

CATBIRD PRESS

First edition

CATBIRD PRESS
16 Windsor Road, North Haven, CT 06473
800-360-2391; info@catbirdpress.com
www.catbirdpress.com

Our books are distributed by Independent Publishers Group

This book is a work of fiction, and the characters and events in it
are fictitious. Any similarity to real persons, living or dead, is
coincidental and not intended by the author.

Versions of "Justice Beyond" and "The Black Hole of Belugessi"
originally appeared in *The Student Lawyer*

Library of Congress Cataloging-in-Publication Data

Kanter, Arnold B., 1942-
    The handbook of law firm mismanagement for the 21st century / by
Arnold B. Kanter ; illustrated by Paul Hoffman.-- 1st ed.
        p. cm.
ISBN 0-945774-57-5 (alk. paper)
1. Law firms--Humor. 2. Lawyers--Humor. I. Title
PS3561.A477 H355 2003
818'.5402--dc21
                                2002015144

For Carol
My managing partner
in fair weather, and foul

Contents

Survival of the Unfittest

Why study law firm mismanagement? Well, if you ask that question (as somebody just did), you are probably unfamiliar with the old saw that "he who does not study history is doomed to repeat it." In this day of heightened competition among law firms, in what has aptly been called a muskrat-eat-muskrat world, it is crucial for the law firm that would survive (and which law firm would not like to do that, eh?) to avoid the trap of old mismanagement techniques by developing and utilizing the newest and best mismanagement techniques.

As Darwin predicted in one of his very long tomes that very few people have the patience to read, only the fittest survive. Competing species – and surely law firms are species – will tend to deviate in order to find their survival niche. Thus, if one observes closely the beaks of finches in certain islands of the Galápagos archipelago through seasons of drought and heavy rain, one will note that the shape and length of those beaks will change according to the availability of certain types of food and the accessibility of that food to various types of beaks. Guppies will do something like that, too, in other circumstances. And though most law firms neither have beaks nor swim, that hardly makes them immune from the forces of evolution.

To summarize, fit law firms – firms that are well managed – will survive in their niche. Unfit firms will scramble to maintain their existence by seeking a different sort of niche, the most mismanaged. Since most law firms, as a species, are not well managed, the competition among mismanaged firms is ferocious. So if you want to get a toe up in the struggle to survive through effective mismanagement, you'd best read this book real carefully.

Law As a Business

Form and Function

Fairweather, Winters & Sommers' consultant, Andrew Tellem of Tellem, Whathey, Noh, addressed the Executive Committee recently on the subject of "Restructuring, Reordering, Redoing, and Otherwise Revamping the Firm's Organization, Structure, Governance and the Like." His remarks are set forth below.

Gentlemen and Gentlewomen:

As you know, we have been undergoing an extensive review of your firm's organizational structure over the past three and a half years. This kind of review inevitably raises emotional issues, since change is never easy and basic changes such as the ones we are talking about are bound to elicit strong reactions. It would serve no useful purpose to revisit all of those reactions here. Such a review would serve only to open old wounds, which are better left to fester. I am sure that both you and we regret some of the verbal abuse, and physical objects, that we hurled at one other. From the standpoint of my consulting firm, I would just like to say that we are prepared to let bygones be bygones.

I think it would be useful to put this review into historical context. Not so terribly long ago (seems like only yesterday, I'm sure), you were a firm of forty lawyers, specializing only in corporate law, and located on one floor of a building in downtown Chicago. Today you are a firm of more than 750 lawyers, practicing in virtually every substantive area of the law, with offices in five cities domestically and three abroad. To use a technical phrase, you've obviously come a long way, baby.

This growth has necessitated creating an infrastructure to support your operations. And as you added new practice areas, it became necessary to divide into departments. Your initial division into "Corporate" and "Not Corporate," while perhaps sensible, was hurtful to the Not Corporates, who felt that they deserved more respect. Fortunately, this was easily resolved with a simple name change. Would that all organizational issues you have faced could have been resolved so easily. Alas and lackaday.

In the interviews that I conducted with your partners in connection with this work, I found considerable confusion as to the roles of the Practice Groups and Industry Groups that you have formed at our behest. Often this confusion was expressed simply in questions such as "What's a Practice Group?" or "What do you mean by an Industry Group?" In other cases I found a far richer, more complex confusion as in "Yes, our group practices with great industry in our department."

In deciding to create the Practice Groups and Industry Groups, we asked whether form should follow function, or function form. After wrestling with this question for several months, we decided in the end that the answer to that question was "yes, but not slavishly."

It may be worthwhile for me to reiterate for you some of the reasons we created the Practice Groups and Industry Groups. As you know, with your growth in size the departments became unwieldy for certain purposes; let's be honest, for most purposes. The Practice Groups were a way of providing a more manageable size for running your business and of fostering the type of specialization the market demanded. For associates it was also a way of assuring that they did not get lost in the larger size of the firm. Unfortunately, this effort to prevent associates from getting lost has not been entirely successful. In fact, Nails Nuttree, who as you know is Chair of the litigation department, asked me to inquire if any of you knew the whereabouts of Jamie Stentson, a third-year associate who was last spotted some four months ago in the library. Nails was unable to provide a description of Jamie and, in fact, was not completely sure whether Jamie was male or female, though he said he was "about seventy percent sure that Jamie's a boy."

The formation of the Industry Groups was pretty much a ploy of the marketing department. They thought that being able to go to a client and talk about your telecommunications industry group would convince clients that you were experts in that area. Of course, to make this work you needed to have within the Industry Groups people from different Practice Groups and Departments. This has created a few of what I'll call "turf problems." For example, exactly who has authority over little Jamie Stentson, should he or she be found again, the litigation department into which Jamie was hired, the complex litigation practice group of which he or she is a member, or the pollution industry group of which Jamie is a part? Come to think of it, this confusion may account for Jamie's apparent disappearance.

You may understand this better if we analogize the Departments, Practice Groups, and Industry Groups to the military. In the armed forces, we have battalions, regiments, platoons, companies, squadrons, garrisons, troops, units, brigades, corps, phalanxes, and divisions, each of which has a particular purpose. No, never mind, I guess that analogy doesn't help all that much when you get right down to it.

Of course, overlaid on all of this is your office structure. The office, being a physically distinct entity, is and always has been a natural governing unit. For example, your firm has nice bouquets of flowers on the reception desks of your offices. It makes good sense for the purchase of these flowers to be handled locally. Recently you have come to this conclusion as well and stopped shipping flowers weekly from Chicago to the other offices. I congratulate you on this recognition, and on the formation of local Floral Committees in each of your offices to coordinate both the purchase and the arrangement of the flowers.

Within each office unit, of course, you have members of the various Departments, Practice Groups, and Industry Groups. This is what I refer to as the underlay to the overlay of the office structure. What we have is a kind of matrix management. To understand this, you need to move beyond the typical organizational chart with boxes and lines of authority, and be able to visualize a 3-dimensional sphere or cube in which lines intersect to reflect the complex multi-level managerial structure that you now have in effect.

Perhaps it would be easier to envision the Firm as a watermelon. The outer green skin is the Firm itself. The inner white shell might be the Executive Committee. Of course, you can slice a watermelon, or a firm, in many ways. You can cut it in two, either the long way or across the fat middle. If you did this, the two pieces you have left might be thought of as the Firm's old "Corporate" and "Non-Corporate" departments, or perhaps as the original Chicago office and the second, New York office. But in your organizational structure you have gone way beyond this type of gross cutting in half. Imagine round slices, or perhaps some juicy wedges. Now, let's be honest, with a sharp knife some of the slicing you do is probably going to harm the seeds; let's imagine that the seeds are associates. Some of the seeds may even fall on the floor and get lost, like poor Jamie Stentson. But ultimately, on a nice hot day, you've got yourself a very refreshing dessert, and for not very much money either, especially if you buy the watermelon on sale.

In short, what you have created is a complex organism in which several levels of governance overlap and underlap to form a seamless web of organizational controls that keep your firm, or watermelon, on track, or on the plate. To date, it would not be totally accurate to categorize the Fairweather, Winters & Sommers web as seamless. But that will come in time, much as all good things will, if you have patience.

And speaking of patience, I can see by the old clock on the wall that my time is about expired. In my few remaining moments I would like to paint for you what I see as the future of law firm organization and governance. Over the past twenty years, the organization and governance of large law firms has become increasingly complex. Growth in the size of firms has necessitated adding layer upon layer of management, all of which has redounded greatly to the benefit of consulting firms such as mine.

But there is such a thing as regression to the mean. This is a concept that I don't really understand, but basically it seems to mean that when things have gone too far, somebody's going to stand up and say, "Okay, Charlie, enough of this crap." My prediction is that law firms are going to go back to the good old days when giants roamed the earth. They will do away with all of this structure and select a King (or Queen) to reign and tell his or her subjects what to do. And with that prediction, I would like to yield the floor back to Good King Stanley the First, long may he reign. God save the King.

I Now Pronounce You

Herbert Gander called the meeting of the Firm's newly-named Medium-Range Planning Committee to order.

"I question whether we have a quorum," announced Sheldon Horwitz.

"Sheldon, how can you question a quorum, when everyone on the committee is here, except Sylvia?" asked the Chair.

"I'm prepared to lose, Herb. I'm just exercising my right. If you leave rights unexercised, you're in danger of their atrophying, like an unused leg."

"Sheldon's got a point," agreed Harriet Akers. "I remember when I broke my leg skiing, must have been seven, no, maybe nine years ago. I had my leg in a cast for months and it atrophied something awful. I practically had to learn to walk all over again."

"Well, okay, but I'm ruling that we have a quorum."

"Where *is* Sylvia, anyway?" asked Rudolph Grossbladt.

"She resigned," reported the Chair. "She felt that medium range was neither here nor there, and she wanted to be a part of a committee that was in one of those two places."

"I actually like medium range," volunteered Sheldon. "It's not so long range as to be irrelevant, nor so short range as to be important."

"I'm glad you like it, Sheldon," said Hiram Miltoast. "Now can we get on to our business? I'm concerned that if we don't find a merger partner soon, there will be nobody left to merge with."

"You needn't worry about that," said Sheldon. "That can't happen."

"I'm glad you're so sanguine, Sheldon, but I'm not."

"Well, let me prove it to you, so that you can rest more comfortably when you go to bed tonight, Hiram. It's true that law firms are consolidating at a furious pace. But let's suppose the most extreme case. Assume that all of the other law firms in the world merged together into firm X, Y & Z. That would still leave firm X, Y & Z for us to merge with."

"Not necessarily. If we don't get on the merger bandwagon soon, our firm may find itself at so much of a competitive disadvantage, we'd be forced to go out of business."

"Why don't we talk about what we'd be looking for in a merger partner," suggested Helen Laser.

"Good idea. I'd say that we'd like a firm that is strong in many different practice areas, especially areas that are hot and profitable, such as mergers and acquisitions," suggested Jim Freeport.

"We'd want a firm with a consistent record of high and growing earnings," ventured Helen.

"And I'd say that we need a firm with an international string of offices in the key financial centers of the world," said the Chair.

"Definitely, and the offices themselves should be classy, too. And, of course, the firm would need to have an unblemished record for quality legal work and for the highest ethical standards," added Hiram.

"And we'd want a place that has a collegial culture, where lawyers and staff treat one another with mutual respect and pitch in to help one another out," said Jim.

"Oh, yes," said Sheldon, "and we'd like the water fountains to spout soda pop, for the sun always to shine on the firm, for all of the women to be beautiful and all of the men handsome, for the people to be diverse in race and religion, and for...."

"Sheldon, you're sounding a bit sarcastic. Is that possible?" asked Rudolph.

"Well, let's put it this way: listening to the characteristics we've been talking about does leave me with a question."

"Let's hear it, Sheldon," said the Chair.

"Why would any firm that met those criteria want to merge with us?"

"We're just coming up with a list of desirable characteristics, Sheldon. We're not saying that our merger partner would necessarily have all of them. And it would be up to us to present our firm in a way that would make us attractive to the merger partner."

"That would require some creativity," said Sheldon.

"Why don't we move on to the question of how we should go about identifying prospective merger partners," suggested the Chair.

"Well, there are various publications that list firms in order of their revenue, or by the number of large transactions they're involved in. We could look at those," suggested Rudolph.

"We could, but every firm in the country is probably looking at those same lists. And Sheldon does have a point. Firms near the top of those lists might not be all that interested in merging with us, unless we became a lot more profitable."

"In which case we might not be all that interested in merging with them," added Sheldon.

"Well, there is one way of identifying firms that are interested in merging," said Hiram. "Every week we read about firms that are seriously discussing mergers, and most of those mergers wind up not happening. If we talked to those firms who've been unlucky in love, we might be able to pick one of them up on the cheap."

"You mean, catch them on the rebound?" asked Jim.

"You might put it that way," admitted Hiram.

"Usually, there's a reason why those marriages don't get made, so we might be picking up the problems that made another firm decide to pass on them," said Helen.

"True, but sometimes the reasons the mergers don't go through are very specific to the particular firms—conflicts of interest or culture clashes—and might not apply to our firm," argued Hiram.

"Yes, but we might invest a lot of time and effort, only to find that the reason the merger didn't go through does apply to us, as well," countered Helen.

"There may be a way to shortcut that," suggested Hiram.

"How would we do that?" asked the Chair.

"Well, consultants often are involved in these mergers. We could engage one of them and perhaps learn, very quickly, what went wrong."

"But wouldn't that be a conflict of interest on the part of the consultant?" asked Sheldon.

"Sheldon, the consultants who do those merger deals work both sides of every deal and trade on the information they learn in one to try to put another merger together. They make the sleaziest of law firms look prim and proper."

"That raises the question of whether we'd approach potential merger partners ourselves, or go through a consultant or headhunter," said the Chair.

"Well, if we approached them directly, that might make us appear weak or overanxious. And besides, it's a bit unseemly, isn't it," said Hiram.

"And it's more seemly and we would appear stronger if we got somebody else to do our dirty work for us?" asked Sheldon. "Besides, employing these people isn't exactly free. They get a hefty fee if the deal goes through."

"Y'know, I've been thinking," said Jim.

"Oh-oh," replied several committee members in unison.

"Maybe we're barking up the wrong merger tree. Inter-law firm mergers have gotten extremely competitive, and they're very hotly negotiated. Maybe we ought to be thinking of merging into some really big corporation, where what they'd be paying for us would be insignificant to them."

"Interesting idea, Jim. But there are a bunch of problems, including ethical ones, that it would take quite a lot of time to work through," said Helen.

"Point of order, Mr. Chairman," interjected Sheldon. "Wouldn't that make it a long-range plan, and so outside of the jurisdiction of our committee?"

"I'll take your objection under advisement, Sheldon, and rule at our next committee meeting. Taking on a long-term project like that would have at least one advantage, though."

"What's that?"

"We might be able to convince Sylvia to rejoin our committee."

Now You See It, Now You Don't

Steven Woo and Jeremy Nelson, former Fairweather, Winters & Sommers associates, were preparing for their meeting with Stanley J. Fairweather, who was due to arrive momentarily. Steve and Jeremy had left the Fairweather firm six months before to form their new venture, Virtual Law Firm.com. While awaiting Stanley's arrival, Jeremy was bringing Steve up to date on the meeting he had had with Stanley the week before, in which Jeremy had tried to explain to Stanley the advantages to the Fairweather firm of becoming a client of Virtual Law Firm.com.

"So then he says, 'I don't get it. Is it there or isn't it there?' I mean, like, these guys totally don't get it."

"Totally."

"So I try to explain it over again to him. You form this virtual law firm. Clients can get access to the lawyer they want, but the firm doesn't have huge expenses, like renting all of this space in a big, prestigious building and stuff. So then what does he ask me?"

"I give, what does he ask?"

"Then where would I sit?"

"No."

"Yes, totally clueless."

"So what did you tell him?"

"On your butt, man."

"No, you didn't."

"No, I couldn't do it to him. He's actually a sweet old guy."

"Stanley Fairweather a sweet old guy? Not."

"Okay, so maybe you're right, but I couldn't say, 'on your butt.'"

"So how did you explain it to him?"

"I told him about the Easter Bunny."

"The Easter Bunny?"

"Yeah, I told him how the Easter Bunny seemed to be there to kids. You could tell them that it didn't exist, but they wouldn't believe you. So I told Stanley that this virtual law firm is a little bit like the Easter Bunny. You can make grown-ups believe that a law firm is there, even when it actually isn't there."

"But it *is* there."

"I know it is, and you know it is, but to Stanley it's like the Easter Bunny."

"So did he accept the idea?"

"No, he said he doesn't believe in the Easter Bunny, apparently never has. And then a client of Stanley's called with an emergency and he said we'd have to reschedule our meeting for today. I suggested that we meet over here, so he wouldn't be interrupted. Oops, I think I hear him coming."

"Hello, Mr. Fairweather."

"Well, well, well, if it isn't the Easter Bunny Boys. Nice office you've got here, Boys. Is this a virtual office?"

"No."

"Good. You gave me a fright there for a second. I thought I was seeing things that weren't there."

"No, this is a real office, Mr. Fairweather."

"I must have misunderstood you. I thought that there wasn't going to be an office."

"Well, sometimes you need a place to meet with clients, like this."

"So there *is* going to be an office. That's good, very good, because I was worried about Marge."

"Who is Marge, Mr. Fairweather?"

"Who is Marge? Who is Marge? Why, Boys, Marge is our main receptionist, has been for over thirty-five years. In fact, she used to be our only receptionist. And if your little idea here means getting rid of Marge, well, forget it. There's not going to be any virtual Marge, I'll tell you that right now."

"Well, this is an example of the kind of cost savings that a virtual law firm would bring. You wouldn't need to hire a lot of people like receptionists."

"Wait a minute, I'm getting confused here. I thought you said last time that we didn't need an office, but here you are, the Easter Bunny Boys, and you've got a real office and you say that sometimes you need to meet with clients. So what's the deal, do we have an office or don't we?"

"I think what I said, Mr. Fairweather, is that you wouldn't need a large, central office. Or at least I meant to say that."

"But clients like to come to law offices to see their lawyers."

"Actually, we've done a survey, Mr. Fairweather, and most clients would welcome not having to go to lawyers' offices to meet with them. They're perfectly happy to deal with their lawyers over the phone, or by email. And when a meeting is really necessary, most of them would prefer that you come over to their offices, anyway. It's more convenient for them."

"What about all of the files, though? We need to maintain them at the office."

"Paper files are getting obsolete, Mr. Fairweather. Most everything is online these days, so everyone who needs them can get easy access to them. And whoever needs to maintain a paper file can do it wherever he or she works."

"How would we keep tabs on people, though? When they're in the office we can see them working. There would be a lot of temptations working at home."

"Actually, studies show that people who work at home are more productive than those who come into a central office. In any event, you'll have ways of monitoring how hard people are working, since you'll still have their time records. And these are professionals you're talking about, anyway. They shouldn't need a lot of monitoring."

"There are times, though, you admit, when it would be necessary to have an office?"

"Yes, but a very much smaller office would do. You could have a small number of lawyer-size offices, say twenty or so, that could be used by people when they needed to come into the office, and some conference rooms for larger meetings. You wouldn't need much more than that."

"So, I could have my own office, with my secretary, Bertha, and Marge could be the receptionist, and we wouldn't have a couple hundred lawyers and staff running around on six floors in two elevator banks?"

"Exactly."

"So it would be sort of like when I started the firm, a small, personal office. We could change the lettering at the entrance from 'Law Offices of Fairweather, Winters & Sommers' to 'Virtual Law Offices of Fairweather, Winters & Sommers.' I suppose, if I wanted to, I could even buy Bertha a typewriter and have her type carbon copies of my letters."

"You could, if you wanted to, Mr. Fairweather."

"Well, Easter Bunny Boys, this is starting to look a lot more attractive to me. We could use your high tech to get back to a low-tech feel, and we could save a bundle of dough in the process. That would allow us to lower our fees to clients, so they wouldn't resent us so much. And it might be a step towards establishing the types of relationships we used to have with our clients twenty or thirty years ago."

"So, does that mean that you're going to become a client of Virtual Law Firm.com?"

"Not so fast, Boys. This is a pretty radical change you're proposing. I'm thinking of a more modest step, to start with, one that is a whole lot safer."

"What do you mean?"

"Well, doing away with our law firm and going to a virtual law firm is risky. Our clients may actually miss having a real law office to go to. But if we start by creating a virtual executive committee, who in his right mind could possibly miss them?"

Nobody's Business

The Fairweather, Winters & Sommers Finance Committee was in session, reviewing the Firm's latest quarterly results.

"Well, it doesn't look good," said Gary Swath.

"Yes, but it's only one quarter," cautioned Hector Morgan.

"True, but if you look at the last *two* quarters, it's even worse," replied Gary.

"Yes, but that's only a half year," countered Hector.

"True, but if you look at the last *three* quarters...."

"Okay, enough," said Committee Chair F. Fred Feedrop. "This kind of talk is not constructive."

"Since when does committee meeting talk have to be constructive?" asked Fawn Plush. "We've certainly never had that rule before, and I would object, because it would stifle conversation greatly."

"Relax, Fawn, I'm not promulgating a new rule, just suggesting that we move things along."

"Fine, then I withdraw my objection."

"Jack, you're our firm comptroller. Don't you have any insights into what's going on here, why our profits are in the tank?" asked Hector.

"Well, actually, that's not my department," answered Jack Figuremeister. "I add, subtract, multiply, and divide. Analysis I leave up to somebody else, which is why we invited our new economist, Dr. Samuelson Ostenhizer, into the meeting."

"Well, what about it, Sam?" asked Hector.

"I do not go by Sam, Hector."

"Okay then, Samuelson, what's the story?"

"I go by Dr. Ostenhizer, to you, if you please."

"Fine, Dr. Ostenhizer. Can you please explain to the committee why our results have been so disappointing over the last year or so."

"First, Hector, I would not say that your results have been disappointing."

"You wouldn't? Well, that's encouraging."

"No, I would say that they have been positively abysmal."

"I see. And how would you explain them?"

"Do you want the macro-level or the micro-level explanation, Hector?"

"Which would I be more likely to understand?"

"I don't like your chances of understanding either, frankly."

"Fine, then give me macro."

"On a macro level, the practice of law has become infinitely more competitive. This means that for a firm to succeed in this market, it must have the top legal talent in the community and it also must be exceedingly well managed."

"And where have we fallen down?"

"On both."

"Well, maybe we should look outside law," suggested Fred. "Many other firms are looking into multidisciplinary practices. Accountants, investment banks, and consulting firms have been encroaching on our turf. Maybe we ought to give them a taste of their own medicine."

"The trouble with that, Freddy, is that those other professions are probably every bit as competitive as law, so you wouldn't be gaining much by going into them," said Dr. Ostenhizer.

"Well, it wouldn't necessarily have to be one of those professions. Our choices are constrained only by the limits of our imaginations."

"Oh-oh," said Gary.

"What's the matter?" asked Fred.

"I'm thinking that if we're limited by the scope of our imaginations, that's a pretty serious limitation."

"Nonsense, you underestimate us, Gary. Now, I think we need to consider entering an industry that is not so competitive."

"But wouldn't a less competitive business mean that we'd have lower profit margins?" asked Hector.

"No, actually, Hector, if an industry is not competitive, it's likely to have higher profit margins," corrected Dr. Ostenhizer.

"I knew it was one or the other, I couldn't remember which. But if there are higher profit margins in less competitive businesses, why doesn't everyone go into less competitive industries?" asked Hector.

"Two reasons. If everyone went into those industries, they wouldn't remain less competitive. And just because profit margins are high doesn't mean that a business will be successful. There may not be sufficient volume to sustain a business."

"Hey, this is really interesting stuff, Dr. Ostenhizer."

"I'm glad you think so, Hector. Perhaps if you'd taken a few econ courses along with your History of Art in the Middle Ages major, you'd be better equipped to contribute to these Finance Committee deliberations."

"I think we ought to get way far away from the law business, say into the automobile industry," suggested Gary. "We could come up with a new prestige car, call it the 'Stanley J.,' after our beloved founder and leader."

"I'm afraid that we have a precedent for that. The Ford motor company named a car after one of the boys, Edsel, and it flopped, big time. Besides, to get into the auto industry would require a capital investment we couldn't begin to contemplate making. So, I think we've got to set our sights on a more modest venture."

"Don't we have a bunch of ethical constraints to worry about, I mean if we bring outsiders, non-lawyers, into a business that practices law? I was under the impression that the Code of Professional Responsibility prohibited that, or at least made it very difficult."

"No, I don't think we're going to have to worry too much about that one, Fred," opined Hector.

"Why do you say that?"

"Well, I anticipated that we might be discussing this issue, so I raised the matter with Steve Mestrow, of our Ethics Committee."

"And what did he have to say that reassured you so much?"

"Well, he said that the Code of Professional Responsibility would definitely prohibit the type of activity we're talking about."

"I don't understand. Why did that reassure you?"

"He reminded me that the Code of Professional Responsibility was promulgated by lawyers for lawyers, and that one of its primary purposes has always been to protect the interests of lawyers. Once lawyers conclude that multidisciplinary practice is in their interest, Steve thought that they would have little trouble unpromulgating any ethical rules that might otherwise stand in the way."

"I'm getting a bit discouraged talking about this whole multidisciplinary thing," said Gary. "Seems to me it's going to be a whole lot of trouble. It's going to require a lot of talents that our lawyers don't have, so we're going to need to hire a bunch of people to carry out whatever we decide to do. And we're already choking with all of the people we've hired, as it is."

"Hang on just a minute, Gary. You gave me an idea."

"I did? What is it, Fawn?"

"Well, as you said, we've already hired a lot of people in different areas to provide a range of services to the Firm—photocopy, secretarial, gym, cafeteria, day care, travel and others."

"Yes, so what, Fawn?"

"What if we just bundle these services together and offer them to people outside of the firm as Fairweather Office and Other Liaison Services (FOOLS)? We wouldn't need to hire anyone else, and we just might have ourselves a nice little business."

Brand New

The Fairweather, Winters & Sommers marketing consultant, TRGLFMCG ("The Really Good Law Firm Marketing Consulting Group"), was called in recently to advise the Firm on marketing issues and issued this confidential report.

Introduction

You engaged TRGLFMCG to evaluate all aspects of your marketing activities to date, and to recommend a course of action to you.

This work has taken longer than anticipated because of the thoroughness with which your lawyers insisted our work be done. For example, to assess your client service efforts, it probably was not technically necessary that we conduct in-depth, in-person interviews with each of the principal officers of all of your clients. This process was complicated by the fact that you are constantly adding new clients (though not any sizable ones) and that some of your former clients decided no longer to be your clients, in part because of our extensive interview process. Nonetheless, it has been a rewarding six years for us, and we respect and admire your firm's attention to detail.

This report is divided into five sections: preliminary analysis; interviews with your clients; rejection of certain suggestions made by your partners; recommendations; and conclusion. Actually, if you are prepared to consider this introduction as a section, which we believe would be totally appropriate, the report is divided into six sections: this introduction and the other five sections we just mentioned.

Preliminary Analysis

In order to develop a marketing strategy, we first had to analyze the strengths and weaknesses of the Firm, and then look at the opportunities that exist in the legal marketplace. To accomplish the first part of this analysis, we conducted interviews with some 56 partners in the Firm. The following is a summary of what we learned.

Strengths. We think that you can best appreciate the nature of the comments we received if we give you some direct quotes from our interviews:

> We have a lot of depth.
> Our breadth is pretty broad.
> We're not as weak as a lot of lawyers at other firms say we are.
> Our softball team finished third this year, and we're still young.
> When it comes to solving problems, we're pretty good.
> We're honest as the day is long.
> Our photocopying operation is second to none.
> We try to help out our clients as much as we can.

As you can see, these quotes—and we've tried to pick out the best—do not present a nuanced assessment that would lead most clients to choose your firm over one of your competitors. You would benefit, we think, from greater specificity and a somewhat more forceful presentation of your strengths.

Weaknesses. Your partners should be congratulated for the candor and enthusiasm with which they identified weaknesses in the Firm. Again, some direct quotes may best demonstrate our point.

> Our litigation department sucks. You're not going to tell Nails Nuttree I said that, though, are you?
> We have been unable to develop a first-class business practice, or even a second-class one.
> Many of our best young partners have been picked off by the competition.

> Our firm leadership lacks any vision; no, actually, they're near-sighted.
> Our partners aren't crazy about working too hard.
> Garbage in, garbage out.

Obviously, these views of your partners have proved something of an impediment in improving your marketing efforts.

The Legal Market. A lack of significant strengths and an overabundance of weaknesses would be less serious in a seller's market. Unfortunately, the legal market can best be summed up in the phrase used by one of your partners, "it's a jungle out there." This highly competitive environment gives you three basic choices:

Option One. Get out there and compete, show them what you're made of, put the Fairweather name out there and prove that you accept second place to none.

Option Two. Wait out the market. These highly competitive markets don't necessarily go on forever. If you can just hang on a decade or two, clients may be falling all over themselves looking for lawyers.

Option Three. Fold your cards.

It is too early for us to recommend a definite course of action to you, but at the moment we are leaning strongly towards Option Three.

Interviews with Your Clients

As indicated earlier in this report, our firm conducted extensive interviews with your clients. Because all of the people we spoke with required complete confidentiality, however, we are unable to report on any of those interviews here. It's fair to say, though, that, taken together, they do not paint a pretty picture. On the other hand, it's encouraging to note that they are consistent with your own assessment of your weaknesses, reported *supra* (consultants can speak Latin, too).

Suggestions Made by Your Partners

Though your partners had little experience or apparent interest in marketing, we found no shortage of strong opinions among them as to what the Firm should do. We consider some of these suggestions in this section.

1. *Hire more marketing staff.* The Firm already has a marketing director with a support staff of six. Given the results that they have produced so far, we see little to suggest that further investment in this area would pay large dividends. We might (and, in fact, do) observe that the Firm's solutions to most of its problems seem to involve hiring a lot more staff, and that this propensity to hire more staff has made the Firm less profitable than it might otherwise be, giving rise to your competitors' success in picking off some of your best younger partners (see the discussion *supra* under *"Weaknesses"*).

2. *Branding.* This is an attempt to make a firm a "brand name," and is one of the hottest areas in marketing (and, therefore, very profitable for us). Because you are such a good client, though, we feel constrained to admit that we don't have a clue as to what branding a law firm would entail. If you nonetheless want to pursue this route, we would be happy to advise you, as we have considerable experience in advising other law firms on this matter.

3. *Develop a Firm logo.* The partner who suggested this pointed out that such a logo could be used on Firm stationery, cups and plates, t-shirts, caps, briefcases and a host of other items. This seems to us a good idea, and we would recommend a logo that draws on the Firm name, perhaps a sun melting a snowman into a swimming pool. Logo development seems like a perfect occasion to create a Logo Subcommittee of your Marketing Committee.

4. *Name a stadium or sporting event.* The partner who suggested this said that he had in mind the Fairweather, Winters & Sommers Super Bowl, or the Fairweather Yankee Stadium. We have looked into this possibility and ascertained that the cost of

such a naming would account for projected Firm profits through the twenty-third century. This does not mean that the concept is not a good one, however. We are exploring what attaching the Firm name to the new outdoor luge stadium that is in the early talking stages in Miami would run.

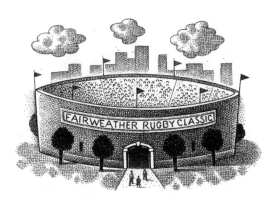

Recommendations
We think that the work the Firm has done so far has made important progress in identifying Firm weaknesses, raising insoluble issues, and shooting down some of the harebrained ideas suggested by your partners. It has also been an important and steady source of income to our firm. As much has changed in the six years since our work commenced, we think that it is time for a reconsideration of the matters discussed in this report, and recommend that you engage us to spearhead that reconsideration.

Conclusion
Successful marketing does not come easily. Although your efforts to date have been futile, you are to be congratulated on your persistence and willingness to invest in our services. We hope and trust that in another six years we may have a rosier picture to paint for you.

See No Evil, Hear No Evil, Speak No Evil

Fairweather, Winters & Sommers' largest client, Endrun Corporation, came under scrutiny recently for questionable accounting practices that critics charged had overstated the corporation's earnings by an average of $17 billion a year for the past eight years through a complicated scheme that involved putting all of its expenses on a competitor's MasterCard. Endrun asked the Firm to look into the allegations of misconduct and to issue a report on its findings. The Firm's Ethics Committee members debated whether the Firm should accept the engagement.

"I don't get it," said Stephen Mestrow. "Endrun is our biggest client by a factor of three. They ask us to do some work for them, we do it."

"Not necessarily," argued Ellen Jane Ritton. "If your largest client asked you to commit fraud, would you do it?"

"Probably not," said Stephen.

"*Probably* not. You mean that you might?"

"Well, what do we have malpractice insurance for? We pay these incredible premiums and we never get a payoff."

"Our insurance policy wouldn't cover fraud, in any case," pointed out Chair Patrick Conshenz. "That would be excluded."

"Oh, in that case, no, I definitely would not commit fraud, even for our largest client," said Stephen. "Not if it isn't covered by insurance, no way."

"Well, I'm glad to see that you have such high principles."

"I don't know why we're talking about fraud, in any case. Where in this proposed engagement does it ask us to commit fraud?"

"Of course they're not going to ask us, in an engagement letter, to commit fraud. It's just the whole circumstances don't really smell right to me," said Mary Ellen.

"Oh, I see. We should turn down an engagement by our largest client, who has paid us legal fees of over $12 million dollars a year, because it doesn't smell right to you, Mary Ellen? Is that what you're saying?"

"I'm saying that when something doesn't smell right, you've got to be careful."

"I thought this committee was entrusted by the Firm with using its brain to make decisions, not its nose."

"Well, Endrun is all over the press these days," said Lydia Milife. "It might not be the best thing in the world for us to get involved in."

"Since when did we shy away from taking matters on because they may be unpopular? Sheldon Horwitz is representing a mass murderer who tortured his fourteen octogenarian victims before killing them by playing a tape that asked why their children never call them anymore. We'll probably spend 2000 hours on that case and not get paid a red cent, but we shouldn't take on Endrun?"

"We don't have a potential conflict in Sheldon's case, Stephen."

"Well, I don't get the conflict that we have in this case, Lydia."

"How about the fact that we've been paid enormous fees by them in the last four years, and the close relationships we have with Endrun in many different ways."

"No problem. We just disclose them in the report."

"Wouldn't we be better off just telling them that it would be better for them and for us if they got somebody else to do this review?"

"Right. And they wind up hiring one of our principal competitors, that competitor does a good job, and all of a sudden we're out the representation of our largest client, all because of Mary Ellen's nose."

"Y'know," interjected the Chair, "this all could be a tempest in a teapot. It might be that we would conduct the investigation and produce a report that was above reproach and raised no real ethical difficulties at all."

"Unfortunately, though, Pat, we won't know that until we've done the investigation and written the report, will we? It's a little tough to know at this point."

"Actually, I think Patrick is on to something," said Stephen. "I do happen to have a draft of the report, which I could let you all see."

"You've done the report, and you haven't begun the investigation?"

"Don't get excited, Lydia. I said that it's just a draft."

At this point the Chair called a fifteen-minute recess for committee members to read the draft report, which is set forth below.

To: Board of Directors, Endrun Corporation
From: Fairweather, Winters & Sommers
Subject: Report on alleged hanky-panky

INTRODUCTION

Endrun Corporation (hereinafter, "Endrun," "the Corporation," "the Company," or "the Alleged Wrongdoer") has been accused by certain people and governmental entities (hereinafter, "the Accusers") of intentionally overstating its earnings over the last eight years by a total of some $136 billion in order to defraud certain lenders and investors into thinking that the Corporation was in good shape, when, in fact, it wasn't. Wanting, as Endrun CEO Fritz Frankfurter said, "to get to the bottom of this gesh durn thing once and fer all," Endrun has engaged the fine firm of Fairweather, Winters & Sommers (hereinafter "the Fairweather firm," "the Firm," "we" or "us") to, as Fritz put it, "try to figure out what in the heck's goin' on here."

DISCLOSURE OF CERTAIN MATTERS

Being an honorable firm, we want to kind of lay our cards on the table about certain relationships that could cause others, not us, to question the independence of our investigation. To wit:

1. Endrun is the Firm's largest client, having paid us a whopping $48.4 million in fees (22.7% of our gross revenues) in the last four years, for which we are eternally grateful.
2. Endrun general counsel, Lawrence Highner, is a former partner of us.
3. Endrun CEO Fritz Frankfurter is married to the daughter (little Becky) of our partner Hiram Miltoast.
4. We may have advised the Company on certain matters which we will be investigating in order to determine whether they are fraudulent.
5. Endrun's accounting firm, Art Randerson, is our client, and its general counsel and a key officer play golf each Thursday (weather permitting) with two of our partners.
6. Several members of our Firm's Endrun team are sleeping with several officers of Endrun, though, in most cases, they say it's "nothing serious."

SCOPE OF OUR INVESTIGATION

Endrun has placed certain limitations on our investigation, to wit:

1. We're to stay out of things that are none of our business;
2. We're to take as fact anything an Endrun officer tells us;
3. We're to assume the authenticity of any document presented to us by them;
4. We're not to spend a whole lot of time on this nonsense;
5. Our final report must be approved by Endrun's general counsel prior to our submitting it to the board.

WHAT WE DID AND DIDN'T DO

In keeping with the instructions of our client, we spent a nice couple of hours over a really excellent dinner with Fritz chatting about this whole situation. As far as he's concerned, it's "a whole lot of fuss about nothin'." We could ascertain nothing in the course of our dinner (which included a couple really fine bottles of wine) that would lead us to doubt Fritz's conclusion. Having explored this rather thoroughly with Fritz, we nonetheless took some time out of our busy schedules to shoot the breeze with a few other officers of the Company. All of them appeared to be fine, upstanding individuals who had made a shitload of money on the Company's stock and so, near as we could tell, would have no reason to do anything that could jeopardize their investment.

On one of our partners' regular Thursday golf games with George Stonewall, who is a pretty big muckamuck at Art Randerson, they asked George about certain accounting matters that had been called into question. By the third hole, George had bored them to death with little details that they couldn't understand, so they switched back to talking about football, and decided that they didn't like the Chicago Bears' chances this year, unless they pick up a quarterback and a defensive tackle. We feel that we're entitled to rely on Art Randerson, as the experts in this matter, in any case.

CONCLUSION

Based on the foregoing, and subject to all sorts of caveats and possible exceptions, we think Endrun didn't do anything that any other big corporation in the same situation wouldn't of done. Accordingly, we don't think it would be fair, *ex post facto*, to impose a duty on our client to come up with financial statements that are understandable or sensible.

Having reviewed the proposed draft report, the Fairweather, Winters & Sommers Ethics Committee concluded that there was no reason to pass up a tidy fee, and that they would help out the Firm's old friend and client.

Enough of Mismanagement

Lieutenant-Colonel Clinton L. Hargraves, CPA, the Fairweather, Winters & Sommers Firm administrator, addressed those gathered at the annual "State of the Firm" meeting. Attendance at this event is bolstered by an open bar and elaborate munchies, as well as by Stanley Fairweather's directive that everyone attend. A transcript of Mr. Hargraves remarks appears below.

Ladies and Gentlemen:

It gives me pleasure in the extreme to stand before you as your Firm administrator, a position that I have now held during portions of two consecutive centuries. My topic is "Management of Fairweather, Winters & Sommers Today: A Fresh Look," a title that I came up with on my own and which I think is both rather catchy and accurate. I hope that I may be forgiven a brief stroll down memory lane.

When I came to the Firm only 6.2 years ago (I know it probably seems longer, as I've become something of a fixture, if I may say so myself), the Firm had two directors, a Director of Personnel Matters and a Director of Non-Personnel Matters. I am pleased to say that we are now up to sixteen directors: Director of Budget and Finance, Director of Security, Director of Legal Personnel, Director of Non-Legal Personnel, Director of Illegal Personnel, Director of Beverage and Food Services, Director of Word Processing, Director of Mailroom and Messenger Services, Director of Health Services, Director of Library and Microfilm Services, Director of Information Technology, Director of Paralegals, Director of Public Relations and Marketing, Director of Docket, Director of Copying and Faxing Services, and Director of Hotel and Transportation Services.

I am proud of the eight-fold growth in directorships under my reign, which amounts to adding an average of two and a quarter directors each year. (Though we did not actually add exactly two and a quarter in any one year.) If Firm profits had grown at a comparable rate, my Director of Budget and Finance tells me, our Firm would be, and I quote him here, "sittin' pretty." I know that several of you have expressed the view that had our directorship growth been less meteoric, our profit growth would have been more so, but I think that very few things could be farther from the truth.

As our Firm grows in number of attorneys, we need to bulk up our support staff infrastructure to meet their needs. Perhaps you'll permit me an apt analogy here to demonstrate why this is so. Let's say you're about to build a new house. Your architect—we'll call him Pablo (though that may not be his actual name)—has designed a rooftop patio on the third floor of the house, which affords lovely views of the surrounding area and is large enough for entertaining twenty-eight to thirty-seven guests. Unfortunately, in designing the foundation and walls of your house, Pablo failed to take into account the increased weight that the guests on the patio would bring to the structure. The effect of Pablo's oversight may be to cause the structure to collapse at your very first party up there, with you, your spouse, and all of the guests tumbling tragically to your deaths, or at least to serious injury. So what was Pablo's mistake? To put it in terms of our Firm, not enough support staff. (Personally, I also find a rooftop patio of that size extravagant and unnecessary. I rarely entertain that large a group, and when I do, I like to keep them on the ground.) Let's hope Pablo's got some damn good liability insurance, because we're sure going to sue his butt off, aren't we? You bet.

Of course, it is not enough just to have support staff. If all of our directors were nincompoops, that would not get us very

far, would it? Fortunately, not all of our directors are nincompoops. Several of them are talented people, gifted in their fields.
And those who aren't won't last long; you can bank on that.

We have put our directors through a rigorous management
training course, developed by yours truly, based on my experience. The course is not one in which I lecture at them. No, it
involves videos, role playing, and exercises. For example, in one
role play I ask them to imagine that they are a director at a large
law firm. (Since they are, this does not require a lot of imagination.) I ask them to imagine a situation in which an irate partner
at the law firm comes in and complains to them, in a loud and
obnoxious way, about this or that, and that neither this nor that
is their fault. (Since this happens on almost a daily basis at the
Firm, again, not much imagination is required.) The question I
pose to them is this: how does the director handle the situation?

In the role plays, in which, by the way, I cast myself in the
role of the irate, loud, and obnoxious partner, some of the directors resort to physical violence against the partner (me). I try to
point out the drawbacks to this approach to resolving the problem, which include the risk of physical retaliation by the partner and the near certainty of getting fired on the spot. Some of
the directors opt to deny their culpability and to point out that
the partner himself is responsible for the situation, and pretty
much got what he deserved. In these cases, I patiently observe
that partners in this firm do not make mistakes, so the director
is unlikely to win an argument with this assertion. Occasionally,
a director will tender his resignation on the spot. This, I acknowledge, is a possible solution. Finally, I will demonstrate the
correct response, which is to admit the error of the director's way,
to offer to remedy the problem immediately, to humbly beg
forgiveness, and to promise that the situation will never, ever
arise again.

We are not content, however, to rely on formal management
training to improve the performance of our directors. Instead,
we are using actual job experiences to help them learn. Accord-

ingly, we have hired a videographer to follow each of our directors around the Firm in order to record their on-the-job performance. Daily tapes are reviewed and edited by expert managers, and then played back and critiqued for the director. We believe that the additional cost of this process will be repaid many times over in improved management. While we contemplated doing this for our support staff at all levels, we have opted for a less costly alternative. Some of you may have noticed that when you dial a member of our staff, you now get a recording saying that the call may be monitored for quality-control purposes.

"Where are we headed in the future with your crack management team, Clint?" many of you are probably asking yourselves (or, actually, me, since I'm Clint) right now. Good question. Unfortunately, I cannot now give you an answer to the question. I can, however, give you an answer to the question of how are we going to answer your question. We are going to address this topic at a directors' retreat, which I've scheduled for February 12-18 at The Doral Resort and Country Club. I have entitled this retreat, "The Future of Our Crack Management Team," which I think you all will agree is an excellent title.

Now, if I may, I'd like to try to anticipate a few questions that you may have about this retreat. Why do we need six days for a retreat? Couldn't we squeeze it into, say, half a day? Well, for a retreat to be productive, the participants must develop a degree of comfort with one another that will contribute to a meeting where everyone feels free to say what is on his or her little mind. This takes getting to know one another personally, which is why we have invited spouses, significant others, and children to join us. Since time really flies when you're having a good time, which is the type of time that we anticipate having, we figured that a minimum of six days would be required.

Some of you may wonder why we have chosen to hold the retreat at The Doral Resort and Country Club rather than, say, at a Days Inn. As in deciding the length of the meeting, the planner of this meeting, me, was concerned exclusively with what would make this meeting most productive. I determined that the relaxed setting of the Doral, coupled with its three golf courses, would contribute to the type of atmosphere that would allow us to get the most out of the time we spent.

I deduce from the fact that I see Mr. Fairweather moving his index finger back and forth rapidly in front of his throat that my time is about up. Let me just close by pledging to you a report on the results of our "The Future of Our Crack Management Team" retreat at our next State of the Firm meeting. Good night, and may God bless America and our honorable Firm.

Foreign Capital

A large, wall-sized map of the world covered the north wall of the Fairweather, Winters & Sommers International Conference Room, so named because of the large, wall-sized map of the world that covers the north wall thereof. Secretary General Godfrey Bleschieu, Chair of the Firm's International Committee, strode over to the wall, brandishing his pointer.

"Damn, I found it just the other day," he murmured, half to himself.

"What's the name of the city again?" asked Ellen Jane Ritton.

"Begins with an 'A', I think."

"Oh, that's a big help," said T. William Williams.

"I'm trying, T-Bills. It's not that easy to remember those foreign cities."

"Well, what country is it in?" asked Gary Swath.

"One of those Arab or Muslim or Moslem countries, I think; definitely not in Europe. I think it's just across the gulf from Djibouti."

"You remember Djibouti, but you can't remember the name of the country our office is in?" asked T-Bills, incredulous.

"Sure, Djibouti is easy. I just tell myself to think 'jabout it.'"

"Great, well, which gulf is it across from Djibouti from?" asked Gary.

"It's some gulf right near Africa, I think. Wait a minute, here it is, the Gulf of Aden. That's it. Sure, right between the Red Sea and the Arabian Sea. Yup, Djibouti's just where it was yesterday, bordered by Eritrea on the north and Somalia on the south."

"Fabulous, so where's our office?" asked Ellen Jane.

"Let's see, bear with me, we just cross over the Gulf of Aden here, and boom, we're right smack in Anomynia. And here's Anom, which is where our Anomynia headquarters is."

"Headquarters? You mean we've got more than one office in Anomynia."

"Not yet, but we're always looking for expansion opportunities. And right now we're in the catbird seat. We are the only U.S.-based firm that has an office in Anomynia."

"And just why do you suppose our competitors aren't flocking to Anom?"

"Actually, there are several possible explanations. First, they may not have found it yet. As we just witnessed, it's not the easiest place in the world to locate. Second, they may have had difficulty with the language, as there are about 235 different dialects spoken. Third, they may have had some problem in finding office space. And…"

"What about the fact that there's no business there?" asked T-Bills.

"Now, that could have been a factor, too. But you're exaggerating when you say that there's no business there."

"Well, what did we gross last year?"

"Ah, I'm not actually sure what we grossed, but we're not at break-even yet."

"Why would we have opened an office in Anom, in any case?" asked Gary.

"Well, here was our thinking, as best I can recollect it," said the Secretary General. "We noticed the strong trend to internationalization in law firms. All of our competitors were opening offices in exotic places. But we noticed that the competition in many of those places – like, for instance, London, Paris, Tokyo, Singapore – was very stiff."

"Perhaps there was competition because there was some business in those places," suggested Gary.

"Now that's a pretty snide remark, but I'm going to ignore it. Anyway, we didn't relish jumping into a highly competitive market abroad, so we decided to make a trade-off. We'd accept a country with no business in exchange for the opportunity not to have to compete for the business that didn't exist there."

"We opted to become a big fish in a small pond," offered Ellen Jane.

"Exactly," said the Secretary General.

"I'd say a big fish in a dry pond," said Gary.

"There you go with your sarcasm again. It's easy to second guess, with the advantage of hindsight. We've just had some tough breaks this year."

"Such as?"

"Well, first off, the lack of electricity made it difficult to fully integrate our computer system so as to present a seamless appearance to any clients that we might have attracted."

"Wasn't that entirely predictable."

"Sure, in hindsight. But the Office Committee was used to locating offices in the U.S., where you don't exactly focus on the question of whether there's electricity."

"Or water."

"Okay, that was an oversight, too; I'll admit it. But there were other problems that set us back, which we could not necessarily have anticipated."

"For example?"

"Well, shortly after we solved the electricity and water problems, we were visited by a group who impeded our ingress and egress."

"You mean the entire office was taken hostage?"

"'Hostage' is such an ugly word that I don't like to use it; but, yes, I suppose you could say that we were taken hostage."

"And why did they focus on us?"

"Well, the fact that we had electricity and water made us a highly desirable target."

"Have we solved the hostage problem now?"

"Yes. There was a bit of a ransom involved, and that aggravated our failure to make projections."

"And how do we know we're not going to be subject to more ransoms?"

"I think we've got that under control. Unfortunately, that necessitated building up a rather substantial security force to protect the office, which also was an expense that we hadn't anticipated."

"So have we solved all of our start-up problems now?"

"To be perfectly candid, I'd have to say that there are a few kinks we're still having to work out."

"What kind of 'kinks' are we talking about?"

"Well, there are some cultural kinks. For example, our women lawyers are not crazy about the idea of having to wear veils and cover every inch of their skin. The concept of 'business casual' has not taken hold yet in Anom."

"Is that all?"

"No, their idea of pro bono is a bit different than ours in the States. They didn't take so kindly to one of our young associates volunteering to defend a young man whose eyes were going to be put out for having looked at the wife of another man. Apparently, they don't share our notion of cruel and unusual punishments."

"This looks like a disaster, Godfrey. Why don't we just cut our losses and get out of there?" asked Gary.

"Well, there's a little bit of a problem with that, too. It seems that the Anomynia government needs to approve the cessation of business of any foreign nationals."

"So we're stuck there?"

"You could say that, but I think we've taken an important step recently that will help us to develop quite a bit of business."

"And what's that?"

"Well, we've hired a law student who has a lot of potential."

"A new associate is going to develop enough business to make us profitable?"

"We're bullish. Abdul is a son of the king."

"We hired a prince of Anomynia? Is he qualified?"

"Top half of the class at Anom School of Law, Anomynia Jurisprudence Award in Torts."

"Well, that ought to make things go more smoothly."

"We're hoping so, but our new associate arrives not entirely without baggage."

"Yes?"

"Abdul insists that partners call him 'Your Highness.' And we're going to have to expand our offices quite a bit, because Abdul needs space for some of his favorite animals and wives. He's insisting on taking three associates as part of his harem."

"This sounds like another disaster in the making. What happens if we have to fire Abdul?"

"Well, I don't see that as a problem. The King has called us over to the palace to chat, and I think there's a hell of a good chance that young Abdul is going to make partner next year."

Giving the Devil His Due

"Whew, it's hot," said Everett Stokes, wiping his brow.

"Of course, it's hot. You're in Hell," said a fellow with a red suit and a long tail.

"We're in Hell?" asked Mary Flange. "Whatever for? And how do you know where the hell we are, anyway?"

"I know because I am the devil. I reside here through all eternity. And you will all be doing the same, so I suggest that you get used to it."

"But what did we do to deserve this?" asked Arthur Oshten, visibly upset.

"Yes, I certainly didn't do anything," said Jessica Toiute.

"Nor I," added Richard Frentch.

"Well, let's see. We all certainly have plenty of time on our hands, don't we?" said the devil. "Why don't we see if we can figure out why you're all down here. What did you do in the WA, Everett?"

"WA?"

"Yes, World Above."

"I was a lawyer, a partner in a large law firm."

"I was, too."

"So was I."

"Hey, me too."

"That makes all five of us."

"Aha," said the devil, "so we seem to have a common denominator here. All of you were partners in large law firms."

"Yes, but surely that doesn't explain our being here," protested Jessica. "It can't be that all partners in large law firms wind up in Hell, can it?"

"No," admitted the devil. "But it gives you a pretty good crack at landing up down here. Let's explore further. What kind of work did you do?"

"I represented the tobacco industry," said Jessica. "Our firm fought off all of those governmental entities and do-gooders who wanted to deprive the common people of their inalienable right to die from lung cancer."

"My biggest clients were in the firearms business," said Richard. "We tried to prevent the crazies who wanted to take away the constitutional rights of the many fine hunters in our country to carry unregistered semi-automatic weapons."

"I represented industries that might have let just a teeny-weeny bit of sewage slip into streams – just barely enough to make the water unsafe for drinking – and occasionally emitted deadly contaminants into the air, totally by accident, of course," said Arthur.

"My specialty was representing members of organized crime, trying to get them a bit more organized, and fighting off dangerous incursions into their civil liberties," said Everett.

"And I worked with the lumber industry to provide the wood and paper that our country needs so badly, and to ward off those who would object because some dumb bird happened to be endangered or a couple of million acres of parkland might be lost for hiking. I mean, big deal," said Mary.

"So all of you were on the side of the, ah, let's just say on my side of the issues," said the devil.

"I object to that characterization," said Everett.

"Me, too," said Jessica. "Everyone's entitled to representation."

"Yes, that's what they taught us in law school," said Arthur. "The legal system works because everyone has a lawyer, and it's a lawyer's duty to represent his client's interest zealously, without some preconceived notion of right or wrong."

"And it's not fair to associate the lawyer with his client or his client's position. We're just doing our job," complained Mary.

"You mean you actually swallowed those lines?" asked the devil.

"But that's what we were taught in law school," protested Richard. "Representing the unpopular client is as American as apple pie, and we shouldn't be tainted by that representation. Do you mean that it doesn't work that way?"

"Well, let me ask you this: if somebody, let's call him Herbert, was beating the bejesus out of somebody else, let's call him Wesley, and somebody came to the aid of Herbert and helped smash the hell out of Wesley, would it be fair to taint that somebody with Herbert's position?" asked the devil.

"But that's very different," protested Jessica. "We're not beating somebody up; we're just practicing law."

"That distinction may cut it in law school," said the devil, "but it strikes me as too fine a point for us normal folks."

"Really? You mean we're being tagged with our clients' positions and sent to Hell because of that?" asked Everett.

"It's hard to say for sure," said the devil. "But look around you. Do you see any of the lawyers who were representing the other sides of the cases you were involved in?"

"No, not off hand. But it would have been very difficult for us not to take on those cases," said Everett.

"Why's that?" asked the devil.

"Because they were extremely lucrative."

"Yes, our firm did an analysis of our revenue and profit, and found that 31% of our revenue and 47% of our profit came from representing clients on your side of issues," said Arthur.

"And what made those representations so lucrative?" asked the devil.

"For one thing, those clients were always getting into trouble, so they guaranteed a good, steady flow of work," said Jessica.

"And for another, the cases against those clients typically threatened their whole method of doing business, so the stakes were high enough that the legal fees involved tended to be in-

significant to the client, however high they might be," added Everett. "So we could charge top dollar."

"Not only that, the competition for getting those cases was less, since quite a lot of law firms would not dirty their hands by touching them," noted Mary.

"But, if they were so profitable, why didn't every firm in the WA go after them?" asked the devil.

"Not every firm knew how profitable they were," said Jessica.

"And there were others who didn't want to get involved with the kind of clients we were working with," said Mary.

"There was a lot of risk involved, too," added Arthur.

"How so?" asked the devil.

"Well, the government and others were extremely aggressive in going after our clients. And if they were successful, our clients would be put out of business, and the expertise we had accumulated would prove of little use," said Everett.

"So how did you deal with those risks?" asked the devil.

"We tried to plan ahead, to see where the next evildoer might be coming from," said Mary.

"Yes, our firm created a *pro malo* committee to plan our next incursions into the world of the distasteful," said Richard.

"You mean you really did that, created a *pro malo* committee?" asked the devil.

"Well, we didn't exactly call it that," admitted Richard.

"What did you call it then?" asked the devil.

"Our business development committee."

"We had a better way of identifying potential new evildoer clients," said Mary.

"What way was that?" asked the devil.

"We promoted an active *pro bono* committee."

"And how did that help you identify potential new evildoer clients?"

"Simple. We just turned the *pro bono* committee loose, watched who they were targeting for potential lawsuits, and went out and solicited clients in those industries. Worked like a charm," said Mary.

"Well, Mary, I'm not so sure about the rest of the group, but you have clearly come to the right place," said the devil.

Economically Speaking

Recognizing the importance of understanding and staying abreast of developments in the world economy, the firm of Fairweather, Winters & Sommers recently hired its first fulltime economist. Dr. Samuelson Ostenhizer, Felix and Matilda Hobson-Choice Professor of Economics, Emeritus, at the University of Chicago, was chosen because of his towering reputation in the field of economics and because, now that he's emeritus, he's a lot cheaper than his fully-functioning faculty colleagues. His maiden address to the Firm, entitled "The Economy: A Highly Insightful Overview," was recorded, and an unedited transcription appears below.

Ahem ... I would like to thank Mr. Fairweather for that glowing, but accurate, introduction. My remarks this afternoon will be divided into four or five sections, in no particular order. Since I recognize that those of you listening—attentively, I hope—may have vastly different degrees of economic sophistication, I will try to peg my remarks such that they will be understandable to at least a few of you.

"What is the economy, Professor Ostenhizer?" I am often asked. To me, the economy is like an onion; that is, it has many different layers and it often makes you cry. Take a little of it and chop it into a salad or use it as seasoning and it's a terrific little root vegetable; but get carried away with it and all you've got is bad breath.

Now then, we all have heard much about a "global" or "world" economy. "But what does that really mean, Professor?" people ask me. It means this, I tell them: that when your old grandma goes down to the supermarket and buys a watermelon in Princeton, New Jersey, it has a subtle influence upon the price of crude oil in OPEC. Just follow me. If Grandma buys too many watermelons, it may make her less able to afford taking a car trip to see her granddaughter in Topeka. This untaken car trip may, in turn, lower the price of crude oil, but strike at the heart of the family relationship between Grandma and little Rebecca (assuming that Rebecca is the name of the granddaughter), while making her daughter, Alison, who is Rebecca's mother, happy, because Grandma shouldn't be driving cross country at her age, anyway. Once you begin to understand these complex inter-relationships, you can get some idea of how the laws of economics work.

The gross national product, of course, is key. This national product is the sum of all of the gross state products, which in turn are the combination of the gross city products and the gross country products. Add all of these together, and you can tell just how productive, grossly speaking, we as a nation have been. Typically, this is a really big number, often over 13 digits. (To be totally honest, once a number gets that big, nobody can really grasp it, except maybe Alan Greenspan.) If our gross national product is growing, that's healthy. And if our gross national product is growing faster than, say, the gross national products of Japan, Italy and other countries, well, then, good for us, we may just win the gross national product competition that year, and whoever happens to be president of the United States at that time will get credit and probably be reelected, even though he hasn't a clue what the gross national product is or what he did to make it grow so damn much. Such is politics.

Unemployment can be either too high or too low. Though you wouldn't think that unemployment could actually ever be too low, it can. If too many people are working, then where are the workers going to come from to fuel growth in the economy? Also, who's staying home with the kids? And if nobody's stay-ing home with the kids, they could become "latchkey" kids, who are very maladjusted, or they could get into trouble and develop drug problems, which could make them unemployable and lead to a sharp increase in unemployment, sending it way too high for comfort.

One way of controlling unemployment is through the discount rate, also known as the rediscount rate, which can also affect the money supply. The Federal Reserve gives certain banks a discount on money, which is a pretty good deal. I would buy a lot of money if I could get it at a big discount, but nobody's offered me that deal. These banks will, in turn, rediscount it to other banks, or to Bill Gates. What all of these banks charge each other has a profound, though little understood, effect on how people like you and me behave. Personally, I don't understand why anybody has to lend money to banks. I thought they were the ones that lend it, but I guess sometimes, when money is "tight," maybe banks need to borrow money, just like you and me, though, when it's "loose," they've evidently got no problem.

You definitely want to avoid an inflationary spiral, if you're an economy. Inflation is when things cost more one day than they did the day before, which is pretty much every day, if you ask me. When it gets really bad, then you're in a spiral, which, as the term implies, can have a dizzying effect on the overall economic picture. If this happens, the only thing to do is to real-quick try to create a deflationary spiral, which spins the other way and can right the economic ship of state. Of course, you don't want to overdo it, though, because a deflationary spiral can be as bad for the economy as its sister spiral, since prices drop precipitously, causing the people who own companies to cash in their chips and stop producing, with attendant disastrous consequences for the gross national product, the importance of which I alluded to earlier in my remarks, if you recall.

Either of the two spiral sisters can eventually lead to a recession. A recession happens when for three consecutive quarters the economy sucks. Exactly how bad it has to be for the economy technically to "suck" is a matter of opinion, which is why you get vehement arguments as to whether the economy is in fact in a recession or not. One clear indication that we may or may not be in a recession is when consumer confidence drops. This is measured by a poll of consumers, which asks them whether or not they've got confidence. If more than half of those asked say either "no," or "huh?" we may be heading for, or recovering from, a recession. The people who have the final vote as to whether we're in a recession are the President's Council of Economic Advisors, who are venerable economists with no authority, but who like to meet from time to time to tell dirty economic jokes. A depression is what people with a lot of money go into when there's a recession.

With the economy being a global economy, as I said quite a while ago, it's important to keep your eye on the balance of payments, which measures which country buys how much from which other country. It's not good if, say, we buy a lot more goods or services (goods and services are two sectors of the economy; others are video games and lingerie) from Japan than they buy from us. For one thing, it's not fair. For another, we wind up owing them a lot of money, which the government is forced to put on its MasterCard. Though this earns the government frequent flier miles, which the president can use on Air Force One, it's not good in the long term.

Long term, an adverse balance of payments can lead to a decline in the value of the dollar to a point where you'll get less than a million lire per dollar when you travel to Italy. This decline in the value of the dollar will make it cheaper for people in foreign countries to buy goods produced here, which will lead eventually to a restored balance of payments, if everything were left alone. Unfortunately, though, when Congress looks at an adverse balance of payments, it can get very unhappy, which can lead the "hawks" to implement confiscatory tariffs that help farmers and violate NAFTA. This will allow farmers to raise the price of grains to non-farmers, like you and me, which is one of the reasons why an adverse balance of payments is no good. Left unchecked, these confiscatory tariffs can lead to retaliatory tariffs from other countries, which may eventually lead to isolationism or to war, which generally is very good for the economy.

Needless to say, these things can all have an impact on the stock market. We all need to keep our eye on stocks, which are the little letters and numbers that skim across the TV screen when you watch CNN during the middle of the day, except on weekends, when those little letters and numbers are sports scores. Most important is the Dow Jones Industrial Average, whose nickname is "the Dow." A good way of showing that you are up on the economy is to ask whomever you happen to be talking to "what did the Dow do today?" One does not actually have to ask or to watch the "ticker" to know whether the market is up or down. You can tell when the Dow is up, because well-dressed people walking down the street at noon will be smiling and tossing quarters to homeless people. Other important "indicators" are NASDAQ (which stands for "National Association of Securities Dealers and Quacks") and the S&P 500, composed of five hundred stocks that are both "standard" and "poor."

Well, I see by the old clock on the wall that it's time to wrap up this talk. My next talk, tentatively entitled "What Does All of This Have to Do with Law Firms?" will be scheduled as soon as I figure out the answer to the title.

A Tangled Web We Weave

The following e-mail message was sent recently by the new Fairweather, Winters & Sommers Webmeister, Harold Webb, to all Fairweather attorneys, with a copy to all secretaries and paralegals.

Dear People:

It gives me considerable pleasure to bring you up to date on certain new developments on the Firm's website! First, I want to acknowledge that the changes we have made would not have been accomplished without the support of many (too numerous to name) around the Firm. Without their support, we would have accomplished something a whole lot sooner, and easier. But that's water over the dam now, and I don't want to dwell on negativity. I prefer to focus on positivity, instead. The main thing is, we're up and running! Warm congratulations to us all on entering this century!

You have noticed (or will, pretty soon) that this is a rather long email. Normally, I would have sent this to you as an attachment; however, in view of the fact that a substantial majority of our partners have not yet mastered locating attachments, I have incorporated it into this e-mail. File-finding is an area in which we have an improvement opportunity, isn't it?!

We still have the odd kink to work out. For example, several departments have complained to me that their descriptions on the website are not as long as that of other departments. Corporate is unhappy that Litigation has 423 more bytes (actually, their complaint said "bites") of information than their section. Likewise, real estate and estate planning, which I like to refer to together as "the estates," feel that the shrift they have gotten is short. Similarly, various partners have hinted that matters they are working on are more worthy of specific mention on the site than "the piddling little deals" of other partners we currently describe.

Now, I don't want to downplay the seriousness of these concerns a bit, but we do have much bigger fish to fry. I know you will all recognize that it is impossible to assure that each department gets what it considers its fair share of space on the site. We have considered allocating space based on the relative profitability of practice groups, the revenue generated by those groups, or the number of lawyers in the groups, but have rejected such a formulaic approach as cumbersome and inappropriate. Instead, we have opted for a more flexible and informal system of space allocation—Stanley Fairweather decides. If any of you have a problem with that, please let Stanley know what firm you will be relocating to.

There does seem to be a need for coordination within departments, however. Accordingly, we have appointed a Coordinator of Website (COW) for every department, whose job will be to milk all they can in website content from the work of their department. It will be each COW's responsibility to graze around his or her department, gather information, and pasteurize it to make it safe for website consumption.

We have noticed a great variance in the styles and, frankly, in the spelling acumen of the departments. The flowery claims of litigation success do not mesh nicely with the more factual description of our corporate and securities transactions. And while the attempt at poetry by the tax department was certainly well intentioned, it did not blend. Since we want to project an image of "one firm" (whether that image is accurate or not), we have hired a writer to give the site a uniform style and to translate the turgid prose most of you favor into something that should prove more readable to real people.

Several of you have commented to me that you would like to see changes in the section of our website that contains attorney biographies, complaining that our limited and uniform biographical information was "cramping your style," or not showing you off to the best advantage. I understand that many of you are proud of the honors you were awarded in grade school and summer camp, but we had to draw the line somewhere. And trust me, we intended no offense to the animal rights advocates in the Firm by deciding not to include information on pets and by excluding them from appearing with you in your web photograph, even though we know that they are very, very important to you.

We also have encountered difficulty in reaching agreement on music for the site. Several of the partners have expressed a decided preference for classical music selections to reflect an appropriate dignity. Some of our younger attorneys, on the other hand, feel that a fresh and modern approach to music is necessary to attract business in today's world. Still another faction thought that we should choose particular pieces that would give the message we wanted to clients, such as "Everything's Coming Up Roses" or "You've Got the Whole World in Your Hands." I am pleased to announce that we have reached a compromise, and the site will feature exclusively oldies-but-goodies by the Ink Spots.

I suspect that you all are aware by now of the embarrassing episode involving our website. I know that many of you did not think it funny when "litigation juggernaut" was changed to "litigation lug nut," nor did you chuckle when "the firm's successful public offering on behalf of client Fruit of the Loom" became "the firm's successful pubic offering on behalf of Fruit of the Loom." (Several of you with senses of humor actually got quite a kick out of these witticisms.) While initially we suspected that these errors were the result of poor proofreading, we now have credible evidence to suggest that these and other changes were the result of a vicious, demented hacker who gained unauthorized access to our website. Our new security chief, Major Richard Hawkins, ROTC, is on top of this problem, and we expect that we now have it under control.

To assess the effectiveness of our website, we recently convened a focus group of consumers of legal services to give us their candid comments on the site. While, to my mind, their comments were a bit too candid, we have taken them to heart and are planning to implement changes to obviate the problems they identified.

We now plan to include the Firm's address and phone number on the site, an oversight that, in retrospect, I probably should have caught myself. We also are going to make our site more "user friendly." For example, a guest will soon be able to switch from one portion of the website to another, without closing their browser. Finally, we are now more mindful of the need to update our information frequently. One focus group member pointed out that we were touting the services of a partner who, though extremely talented, had left the Firm several months ago to join a competitor. These changes, and others we will be making, are part of our continuing commitment to making the Fairweather, Winters & Sommers website a pretty damn good website!

We welcome your ideas, even though we may decide to reject some of them. For example, the proposal by one partner to allow potential clients to request free answers to legal questions by clicking on our site was clever, but presented certain problems, including potential conflicts of interest and liability for our answers. Our Finance Committee also pointed out that we are in the business of providing answers to legal questions for money, and that offering that advice for nothing could chill clients' desires to engage us on a fee basis. That, they thought, would be unfortunate.

I want you to know that we are on the precipice of introducing some changes that we expect will revolutionize the use of the website and bring us much wealth. I can't tell you about these exciting changes, as they are "top secret." Oh, what the heck, I can tell you a little, if you promise not to say anything to anyone else, okay? Okay.

We are introducing links to commercial websites and will derive a portion of the profits from sales generated through those links. For example, a guest reading about our real estate department soon will be able to click and, presto, he'll be in a position to order a copy of Herb Gander's fine tome, *Possibilities of Reverter for the 1980s*. We are also exploring the possibility of partnering with our clients by creating pop-up ads that will appear when our guests least expect them.

So, as we face the future, you all should know that we are ready for it! Bring it on, say I!

The Last Word

Few things generate as much fear and consternation among senior partners these days as the supposedly recent conversion of law from a profession to a business. Walk into most any luncheon conversation at the local bar association, or cocktail party discussion at which lawyers are plentiful, and you'll hear somebody moaning, "We've become nothing but a business," and another will nod in reply, "Yes, used to be that we were a profession, but not anymore."

To which I say, "hogwash." Law has always been a business. What's changed is that we've *recognized* that we're a business. And a different type of business. Used to be we were a cost-plus business. We figured out how much money we needed (or wanted) to make, added that to our costs, and set our fees accordingly. Thinking was, I guess, that we were somehow entitled to make a comfortable profit regardless of how inefficient we were. Now it turns out that there are some folks who disagree with that notion—our clients.

So that's forced us to become a competitive business. And what's so wrong with that? Competition forces us to be a bit creative. Time was when we liberal-artsy lawyers thought we valued creativity. And competition means we've had to think about what our clients want. That's not so terrible either. What makes us think that we're entitled to operate in a different environment than our clients? Are we better than them just because we went to law school and picked up a few Latin phrases? In fact, I always thought that client focus was part of what made you a profession in the first place.

If it's true that we've lost what we valued as a profession, then shame on us. It's fully within our power to retain (or regain) our professional values. Meanwhile, I sorta like being a business; though, as you've seen in this section, we could perhaps do a little better job of it.

Stanley J. Fairweather

Recruitment

A Whole New Ballgame

Sports mogul and long-time Fairweather, Winters & Sommers client Dennis "Spike" Wilson addressed the Executive Committee, offering them an unusual proposition.

Lady and Gentlemen:

I appreciate this opportunity what you've given me to say a couple of words to all of you today. I been a client of you guys (and gal) for going onto maybe, I don't know, say, roughly twenty or so years, during which time I had the opportunity to observe your team in many different situations. Through my friendship with your general manager, Stanley J. Fairweather, and one of the real sparkplugs of your outfit, your litigation Chair, Nails Nuttree, I come to know quite a bit about the league that you play in, as well. And it's because of what I observed and come to know that I asked to talk with you today.

At the risk of offending some of you fine folks, I got to tell you that I think you are headed for financial disaster unless you make some fundamental changes. Now you ask me, "Spike, why do you say this?"

I'll tell you why I say this. Let's start with the new players you guys put on your team. You pay them all something like a hundred and fifty grand to start, last time I looked. And you pay them this kind of money for the privilege of investing more of your money to train them.

Now, you'll say to me, "Spike, you pay your ballplayers a lot of money, too, don't you?"

And I'll say, "Sure, we pay them some money. But we've seen them play the game."

The guys we get on our ball club have all played ball before. We've seen 'em play the game that we're expecting them to play, looked at whether we think they're going to be able to hit the curve ball or turn a double play. You, on the other hand, you look at how they can write an exam given by some guy who has no idea what it's like to play law in your league. Let me ask you guys a question: when's the last time a client asked you to write an exam?

If we were choosing our ball players the way you pick your lawyers, we'd put them into a classroom and ask 'em some questions like these here:

1. You're up to bat and the count's 3 and 2 and the pitcher throws the ball outside. Do you (a) bunt the ball, (b) swing wildly at it, (c) call time out, or (d) take a walk?

2. You're playing center field and the batter hits a fly ball to you in medium center, with one out and a runner on third. Do you (a) catch the ball and jog into the dugout, (b) catch the ball, autograph it, and flip it into the center field bleachers to your adoring fans, (c) drop the ball intentionally and try to throw the batter out at second, or (d) catch the ball and throw to the plate?

3. You are a runner on second base, with two outs. Your teammate hits a line drive into right center field. Do you (a) wait for your teammate to reach second base to shake hands and congratulate him on his fine hit, (b) tag up on second base in case the center fielder catches the ball, (c) wait until the ball hits the ground, run to third, and stop to chat with the third-base coach, or (d) take off immediately and try to score.

And any guy who could score well on the exam, we would put him on our team. This would probably seem like a pretty strange way to pick ball players, right? But seems to me that's pretty much the way you pick your lawyers.

Not only have we seen our players play the game we want them to play, we require them to play it in the minor leagues for years. You, on the other hand, bring every one of your bright law students straight up to the major leagues and expect them to play with the top pros without the benefit of minor league experience.

And then, on top of it, you pay them all exactly the same amount of money. You do this, I have been told, because you don't want to discriminate among the lawyers you hire. We in sports, on the other hand, have come to the conclusion that it's okay to discriminate on the basis of talent. Life discriminates on the basis of talent, so we see no real good reason why we should not.

And those lawyers you hire who do turn out to have talent are free to pick up and leave your team immediately. Everybody on your team is a free agent all the time. You advise your clients to tie up their key people with long-term contracts and non-competes, but do you follow your own advice? Hell no.

Anyway, I don't want to be the prophet of doom and gloom here, but I see worse coming down the road. You're at six-figure starting salaries now. Pretty soon you'll be starting your rookies at seven figures. You think not? Which of you guys ever thought you'd be paying six figures?

"So what's going to happen, Spike?" you ask me.

I'll tell you what's going to happen. I seen it happen in baseball, I seen it happen in football, and I seen it happen in basketball. The law sport is in for some major restructuring, and you can either see that coming and benefit from it, or you can hide your head in the law books and have those changes blow you away.

Now I'm not the Oracle at Delphi (hah, you guys thought us sports moguls had no culture, eh?) or I'd be even richer than

I am now, which is pretty damn rich, but here are some of the changes I see coming in the legal game:

1. The profession will be divided into different leagues. This is already happening, but nobody seems to want to recognize it. The leagues won't be called "major" and "minor" leagues, but they will be regarded as such by law students and clients.

2. Instead of wasting millions of dollars recruiting lawyers, the major league law firms will form a lawyer draft, in which they will select players from top law schools around the country. The draft will be televised, with hiring partners from around the country sitting at tables conducting the draft, and large crowds of students watching live from their law schools. Given the increasingly international nature of the practice, the draft will be expanded to include foreign law students.

3. Prior to the draft, picks will work out for the teams in a series of moot court competitions, negotiations, and contract drafting exercises designed to determine the lawyers' talents.

4. Most of the students picked will be assigned to minor league law firms for seasoning before being brought up to the majors later in their career.

5. Law students will be signed to long-term contracts. Eventually, the law students' union will bargain successfully for free agency for lawyers after a period of several years at the firm.

6. Firms will adopt a salary cap per firm in order to allow firms to compete on a level playing field and in order to preserve more money for the partners.

7. There will be complex exceptions to the salary cap, allowing firms to match offers made to their own players who are being lured away as laterals by other firms after they have reached free agency.

8. To further level the playing field and to eliminate the advantages held by big market law firms, the league will adopt a form of revenue sharing among firms.

9. Firms will develop corporate sponsors, and top players will endorse corporate products. (I can see my buddy Nails on

TV, saying, "Hello, my name is Nails Nuttree. I'm head of the Gillette FWS Litigation Department. Before an important Supreme Court argument, I know it's important to look my best, so I use the Gillette quintuple-blade razor for a nice, close shave every time. And it doesn't upset my stomach, either.")

10. Given the increased attention to the legal field shown by best-selling novels, movies, and TV shows, opportunities will abound for new sources of revenue, which will include:

      a. TV revenue from telecasting important court cases and negotiations,

      b. Sky boxes from which rabid law fans can watch court arguments and negotiations live,

      c. Lines of clothing and other products that will bear law firm logos, and

      d. Lawyer trading cards

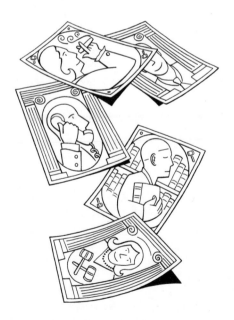

In other words, I see for the legal profession a bright new economic future, if you will only embrace it and take advantage of the opportunities available.

"But talk is cheap, Spike," I hear you saying. "How do we know you are serious?"

Well, Lady and Gentlemen, I'll tell you how you know I'm serious. [At this point, Spike pulled an envelope from his inside sport coat pocket.] In this envelope is an offer from me and a group of investors I have put together to buy the Fairweather, Winters & Sommers firm, and to make your firm the first team to join the ILFA, the International Law Firm Association. In honor of Stanley Fairweather and the practice specialty of Nails Nuttree, your team will be called the Fairweather Torts, and Stanley, if you'd come over here a minute, I'd like you to try on this uniform number 1.

Sex and Practice

Ace hiring partner Sherwood Corrigan, Chair of the Fairweather, Winters & Sommers Hiring Committee, sat at the head of the conference table, his eyes closed and his head shaking slowly back and forth.

"What's the problem, Sherwood?" asked his overworked Director of Recruitment, Annabelle Under-Appreciated, who had just returned from maternity leave.

"What makes you think anything is the matter, Annabelle?" asked Sherwood, opening his eyes.

"Sherwood, you're sitting there shaking your head back and forth – call it a hunch."

"Well, actually, you're right, Annabelle, there is a problem. It's our acceptance ratio."

"What's wrong with our acceptance ratio? We had ten summer associates, made eight of them offers, and all eight of them accepted," said Heather Regale, a recent addition to the Hiring Committee."

"Depressing, isn't it," added Vance Winkle.

"Depressing?" asked Heather. "Why is that depressing?"

"First of all, two of the eight were borderline offers," said Vance.

"What's that mean?"

"Well, we weren't sure whether to make them offers or not, Heather. Their work was okay, but not great. But they were nice kids, so we said, what the hell, and bit the bullet," explained Sherwood.

"Sounds to me like you spat out the bullet and bit the chicken," said Heather. "You took the easy way out, and now we're stuck with them, at least for a year or two. Then, if past history is any guide, we'll do the same thing, and keep them around another year or two, and then probably do it again, until it becomes impossible for them to find a job someplace else."

"Jeez, Heather, you're pretty tough on us today, aren't you, especially for someone who just got put on the committee."

"Maybe I am, Sherwood, but you brought the problem on yourself, so I find it a little hard to be too sympathetic."

"But still, that's only two of the eight. What about the rest of them? Don't we deserve credit for that?" asked Gerry Forspiel.

"Actually, Gerry, though I'm very happy to have the other six, some of my partners aren't so sure," admitted Sherwood.

"Why not? Didn't they ask for them?" asked Heather.

"Sure, we went to the Executive Committee last spring, and the EC told us to hire eight to ten new associates."

"Well, great, we're just at the lower end of their request. So what's the problem?" asked Gerry.

"The problem is that now they're not so sure. A couple of big cases have settled, billings are down a smidgen, so the EC is getting a little nervous," said Sherwood.

"You mean, just because billings are down a smidgen they want to adjust our hiring goals? What's going to happen when billings go up a smidgen-and-a-half next month?" asked Heather.

"Oh, then, of course, they're going to ask why we didn't hire ten, or twelve."

"Maybe we should get them to put their hiring request in writing. Might get them to think about it a little more, and might get them off of our backs later, when they change their minds."

"Not a bad idea, Heather."

"But surely, even if a few cases have been settled, we can use the eight new associates somewhere," said Vance.

"Actually, that's another problem. The students' interests don't fit too well with our needs."

"How do you mean?"

"Well, their interests are about evenly split?"

"You mean between corporate and litigation? That'll work out pretty well, won't it?"

"No, I mean between entertainment law and international law."

"Entertainment and international? We don't do those, do we? How could that have happened?" asked Heather.

"Well, last summer, when we were writing our firm resume, some people were complaining about how ours was not nearly as sexy as some of our competitors in terms of the areas of our practice."

"Maybe that's because we're not in those sexy areas. What did we do, just make things up?"

"Oh, no, Heather, we would never do that. But it did happen that Lou Freeberg had represented a rock star in his contract with a recording studio, so we highlighted that in the Firm resume."

"But Lou's a real estate lawyer. How did he happen to be representing a rock star?"

"The rock star happened to be his wife Trudy's son from her first marriage. Nelson."

"You don't mean Nelson of Nelson and the Nutcakes, do you!" blurted Annabelle.

"The very same. So you know him?"

"Know him? You'd have to be braindead not to know the Nutcakes, Sherwood."

"Well, I guess I just recently became unbraindead then. And, as to the international work, in case you're wondering, Wilbur Jennings happened to negotiate a couple of contracts in Canada for the Strickler Paper Company, one of our long-time corporate clients, so we gave that some pretty good play in the resume, too."

"But, Sherwood, even if you went a bit overboard in the Firm resume, these students were with us all summer. Surely they got a feel for the amount of work we really do in those areas," said Heather.

"We may have misled them a bit there, too, I guess."

"Okay, Sherwood, let's have it. What did we do?"

"You know that as part of the summer program we have these speakers to talk about their areas of practice?"

"Yes, of course I know that," said Heather. "I spoke on 'Developments in Death: What's New in Probate.'"

"I'll bet that was a grabber," said Vance.

"Stop being such a wiseass, Vance. What were you about to say, Sherwood?"

"This past summer, one of our featured speakers was Lou Freeberg, talking about how he landed that $18,000,000 contract for Nelson. And we managed to get Nelson's little brother to perform at the Firm summer party."

"You're kidding. You got the Half Nelson to sing? Cool. No wonder everyone accepted our offers," said Annabelle.

"I thought it was pretty terrible myself, but I guess that could just have been a generation gap. We also had Wilbur Jennings show the slides from the Canadian Rockies heli-hiking trip that he took after the closing of the Strickler deal," added Sherwood.

"So, in other words, we reinforced the notion that we have an entertainment and international practice," said Heather.

"You could say that."

"I did say that. But even if they expressed those preferences, can't we just put them where we need them?"

"It's a little awkward. We practically guaranteed everyone either their first or second choice."

"Fine, so you give them all their second choices."

"That's not so easy. You see, all of the people who expressed Entertainment as their first choice said International was their second, and vice versa."

"But we have booming corporate and litigation practices, don't we? Can't we convince the students to go into those areas?" asked Heather.

"We might have had a chance, except those areas were so busy during the summer that lawyers claimed they didn't have time to use any summer associates. And they were certainly too busy to entertain them. Besides, those aren't the sexy areas, so the students are not real interested in getting into them."

"I've got an idea as to how we might make those areas somewhat more appealing, Sherwood."

"I'm all ears, Heather."

"Ask our former summer associates whether they think it would be better to have a job with some work to do three months after they're hired, or if they'd prefer to be let go from a really sexy area of practice."

Lateraling Out

"And Corporate needs another four," said Annabelle Under-Appreciated, her exasperation showing.

"Your exasperation is showing," commented ace hiring partner, Sherwood Corrigan, astutely.

"How astute of you to notice, Sherwood. Of course my exasperation is showing. That makes eighteen laterals the Firm is looking for right now. Where am I going to find them?"

"Did corporate tell you what they need?"

"Yes, I think they said, 'Four warm bodies, two to five years out, quick.'"

"Well, have you talked to our headhunters?"

"Of course I have, about twenty-two times a day."

"Why so often?"

"Because we deal with twenty-two headhunters, and they all want to talk to me constantly."

"Can't you stop them from calling?"

"Not really. They *do* need information, and if I'm not willing to talk to them, I won't get them to focus on our needs. It's not just me they call, though, it's partners, too. And so I get calls from your partners telling me that Bwana Headhunters has called them and that they've sent over some terrific resumes, which I haven't acted on."

"Well, can't we stop that?"

"Are you authorizing me to screen your partners' calls, Sherwood?"

"No, but maybe I can help by circulating a memo reminding my partners of the procedures we've set up for lateral hiring."

"We circulated that memo three months ago, Sherwood. It doesn't seem to have helped all that much."

"Well, then why don't you tell the headhunters that we won't deal with them if they insist on calling partners?"

"Can we do that?"

"Why not? What kind of response are you getting from the headhunters, anyway?"

"Not great. It seems that everybody in town is looking for laterals."

"So, in other words, the lateral market is as competitive as the law school market?"

"You got it, Sherwood."

"Well, didn't we decide to give our associates some incentive to try to find laterals for us?"

"You mean our Associate Help on Lateral Entry Program, or ASHOLE, as the associates call it?"

"Oops, we probably could have come up with a better name. How's it working, though?"

"I'd have to say, just fair. We've gotten only two referrals, so far."

"Why aren't we doing any better?"

"Well, we're paying $2500 per successful lateral referral; some other firms are paying their associates $10,000."

"Sounds like we may be a bit under market, but I would think our associates would still like to pocket the extra $2500, wouldn't they?"

"Sure, $2500 is better than nothing; but $5000 is better than $2500."

"I don't get it, Annabelle. Five thousand isn't an option. We're paying $2500."

"Think about it, Sherwood. Suppose you're an associate at our firm and you know of a friend—a high quality friend, let's call her Frieda—who is unhappy and would like to make a move. You can make $2500 by referring Frieda to our firm. But you also have a good friend, say, Fred, at another firm that is paying

$10,000 for referrals. If you call Fred and refer Frieda to him, he can collect the $10,000, you split it 50-50 and you walk away with $5000 instead of $2500."

"You've got to be kidding."

"Well, Sherwood, you always say you're looking for entrepreneurial law students."

"Yes, but that's, that's ... treason."

"Oh, come off of it, Sherwood. You're running your firm as a business and you've made a business decision to offer a bonus for referrals. How can you complain when one of your associates takes a better deal?"

"But what ever happened to loyalty?"

"Sherwood, of the eighteen positions we're looking to fill, half of them were caused when two of your partners left the Firm and took a total of nine associates with them. If your associates are looking for models of loyalty, where are they going to find them around here?"

"I think you're being too harsh. There are plenty of partners around who have been loyal to the Firm."

"So far."

"Annabelle, when did you become such a cynic?"

"I just keep my eyes open, Sherwood, and observe. I *was* surprised, though, when three of our associates decided to form a little headhunting firm on the side, because this referral stuff was getting so lucrative."

"How did you find out?"

"They made three crucial errors. They hired one of our secretaries to work for them, part time, at night. And they got our marketing and printing department to design and print their business cards. Here's one, 'Freebish, Contelli & Rousch, Search Consultants.' When I confronted them with it, they said they'd always wanted to be partners in something, and they didn't figure they'd make it at this place."

"You said they made three crucial errors, Annabelle, I only count two: the secretary and the business cards."

"Sherwood, I don't think you want to hear about the third."

"Of course I do. Let's have it."

"Okay, you asked for it. You know that part of our need for laterals has been caused by the departure of some of our associates. Well, three of them have been placed by Freebish, Contelli & Rousch. Rumor has it that they may be kicking back a percentage of their fees to the associates who leave the Firm."

"That's terrible. But how did they convince our associates to leave?"

"That's the saddest part of it, Sherwood. It apparently wasn't very tough. They came up with a slogan that caught on pretty quickly."

"A slogan? What was it?"

"'Fungibility works both ways.' What they mean is that if the Firm treats associates as if they're fungible, then the Firm becomes fungible, too."

"Ouch, that hurts."

"Question is whether it hurts enough to make you want to do something about it. I understand that the Freebish firm has an innovative long-term business plan, too."

"What's that?"

"They plan to re-place their associates every two years at a different firm, collect another fee, then fill the place they've created."

"Why that's a Ponzi scheme. And it's got to fail, eventually, since after two or three moves, the associates will become unplaceable."

"Freebish has got that figured out, too. They expect that some of them will become partners at their last firm, and those who don't can be brought into Freebish, Contelli & Rousch to help with their burgeoning search business."

"This is the most depressing conversation I've ever had, Annabelle. Do you have any ideas for us?"

"Sure, become unfungible."

Well Schooled

Though not yet counted among the elite law schools in the country by the *U.S. News & World Report* annual rankings, a new arrival on the law school scene has attracted considerable attention among college students recently. Students who requested a catalogue from the school received the following letter from the law school's dean:

Dearest Prospective Student:

Congratulations on your decision to explore a career in law.

We believe that no career offers greater potential for personal fulfillment than the one you have chosen. Of course, to be candid, we should say that quite a large number of people disagree with our assessment, many of them vigorously.

Why, you may ask, do we believe this (the stuff about fulfillment potential)? For many reasons. And what, you may well ask, are some of those reasons? We'll tell you.

First, to be perhaps a bit crass, there's good dough in law. Not as good dough as you'd make as, say, a second-string shortstop on a major league baseball team, but then you don't need to stand in front of some big guy hurling a hard object at you at a velocity greater than ninety miles per hour.

Second, law is intellectually challenging. Not as intellectually challenging as, say, teaching the philosophy of Immanuel Kant, but then you don't have to spend your days and nights hanging out with a bunch of weirdo academics.

Third, law affords an opportunity to help other people. Not an opportunity to help other people as much, say, as being a social worker, but see First, above.

Fourth, you will be afforded a great measure of respect by the public. Not as much respect as afforded, say, a brain surgeon, but then practicing law ain't brain surgery.

Fifth, you can quote things in Latin, and people won't laugh at you (well, some will). Not as many things in Latin as a priest, but even senior partners aren't officially infallible.

And those are just some of the reasons that a career in law can be so personally satisfying. There are many others, although we can't think of any right at the moment. We figure that five reasons ought to be plenty, though.

We are aware that many of you will be applying to better-known law schools around the country. We would therefore like to address head-on the question that many of you may be asking yourselves right this second: "With the excellent choices that I am likely to have, why in the hell would I ever choose to go to your school?"

To answer that question, we should first ask, "What do I want to get out of law school; can I get that from your school; and how does your law school compare to others on this?" To assess that, we've prepared a little chart on the next page that we hope you will find helpful.

Looking at the chart, our school doesn't come out looking so darn good, do we? How then can we still say with a straight face that you should come to our school? Two reasons: no tuition and a guaranteed job.

To understand how we are able to offer you these two benefits, we need to go into the history of the founding of our law school. As is true in so many cases, we were born of necessity. Yes, necessity is our mom. And we're not ashamed of her, even a bit.

Large law firms have been faced with a whopping-big problem for years. They have needed increasing numbers of top attorneys and have sought those attorneys from a stagnant pool of law school students. Not surprisingly, this course of events has led to many things, none of them good for large law firms. Large

What You Want	Our Law School	Other Law Schools
a law school diploma	sure, no problem	yes
accreditation	unfortunately, no	yes
stimulating professors	not really	often
prestige	nope	often
nice long summer vacations	no	yes
extracurricular activities	not to speak of	yes

law firms have been forced to wine and dine law students to excess, to pay exorbitant salaries, and to kowtow to the whims of the new lawyers that they hire. To add insult to injury, law firms have found that the overfed, overpaid, and overindulged lawyers they hired are ill-equipped to practice law.

Only one law firm has had the courage to take the proverbial bull by the equally proverbial horns and come up with a plan to generate a new source of lawyers for the firm and better prepare them for the practice they are entering. The result of this courage is the formation of the law school to which you are about to apply – the Fairweather, Winters & Sommers School of Law.

Our firm wanted to find a source of new lawyers that would not be accessible to other law firms. Creating our own captive law school would accomplish that objective. But we still needed to solve two other problems: how would we attract students to our new law school and how would we prepare the students we did attract to practice law in the way that we wanted them to?

We recognized that we would be facing tough competition from law schools that had been around for decades, generations and, in some cases, centuries. So we asked ourselves what disadvantages those schools had that we might take advantage of.

We noted that most of the students who graduated from prestigious law schools emerged saddled with enormous amounts of debt. Indeed, it was this debt that pushed top law students towards firms like ours in order to earn the salaries that would allow them to retire that debt. If we could fashion a school from which students could emerge innocent of debt, we figured that we might stand a chance of luring top law students away from the siren call of the Harvards and Yales of the world.

Easier said than done, though, right? Right. Developing and running a law school is one heck of an expensive proposition. If only there were a way to generate money from law students other than through tuition, we thought. And then it dawned on us that law firms have been losing money on law students every summer, because it's too short a time to train them in. So why not set up a year-round summer program and use that as the basis for training students to practice law and quickly start to generate revenues for the firm?

The more we thought about this, the neater the pieces fell into place. Law firms used to train young lawyers by in effect apprenticing them to older lawyers. The high salaries being paid to new associates as well as the demands of our clients have gotten in the way of that practice in recent decades. With Fairweather, Winters & Sommers School of Law students, however, the firm would not be saddled with the high salaries that have prevented this type of apprenticeship. And clients could be educated as to how the modest billable hour rate they would be paying for law students' time was actually a very good deal for them.

The final piece of the puzzle was the guarantee of a job with the firm upon graduation. We figure that this will be highly attractive to potential law students, since even were they to land a spot in the most prestigious of law schools, they still would be forced to compete for a job—and some of them would fail to get one at a firm the quality of FWS. The Fairweather, Winters & Sommers School of Law takes the risk out of placement.

We think that you probably see by now why the Fairweather, Winters & Sommers School of Law presents a unique opportunity for you as a prospective law student. (If not, you're probably not bright enough to practice with our firm, anyway.) And that opportunity will be getting even better soon. We have on our drawing board plans for the Fairweather, Winters & Sommers School of Business, which will train the future leaders of industry and instill in them the notion that there is no better place to go with their legal problems than to their fellow Fairweather, Winters & Sommers School alums over at the school of law.

We look forward to your matriculation.

> Stanley J. Fairweather, Dean
> Fairweather, Winters & Sommers School of Law

Looking a Gift Horse in the Mouth

The Fairweather, Winters & Sommers Hiring Committee had their thinking caps on. The idea for thinking caps was the brainchild of committee member Alex Pouts, who had become frustrated at the committee's inability to come up with innovative ideas and thought that the caps—red beanies with a white feather and the initials FWS embroidered in blue—might help. So far, the caps had been noticeably unsuccessful in their stated purpose, but had managed to arouse the envy of other lawyers at the firm, all of whom coveted a thinking cap of their own.

"We've got to come up with a new gift idea," said Chairman Rex Gladhand. "Something that will make us stand out in students' minds. The basket of goodies we've been sending them around exam time is getting a bit tired."

"Why do we have to send them anything?" asked Lionel Hartz. "We're paying them a friggin' fortune in salary over the summer, and they certainly aren't earning it. I'd say that's enough of a gift."

"Now, that kind of attitude is not going to be conducive to good relations with our new summer associates," said Heather Regale. "Remember, these are the people who are likely to become our new associates."

"Who will be paid even more than our summer associates, and who won't be earning their salary for several years, either," replied Lionel.

"Now, Lionel, please. You are talking about your future partners here," said Heather.

"I doubt that very much," said Lionel. "If you look at the number of associates we've elevated to partner in the last several years, I'd say the odds are very heavily against it. So why are we showering these kids with gifts?"

"Well, all of the other firms we compete with are sending students gifts," said Annabelle Under-Appreciated, the Firm's recruitment administrator.

"If all of our competitors were jumping off of a cliff, would we jump off, too?" inquired Lionel, rhetorically.

"Absolutely," answered Alex Pouts. "We'd have to, if they did."

"I suppose you're right," admitted Lionel.

"But if we're going to send a gift to them, why do we send it around exam time, after they've already accepted our offer? Why not send the gift before they've made a decision?" asked Alex.

"That would look like a bribe to get them to accept the offer," protested the Chair.

"Uh-huh," said Lionel.

"Well, let's table the question of when we send it. Does anybody have any new ideas for a gift?" asked the Chair.

"I do," offered Heather. "Why don't we pick out a distinct gift for each student, geared to his or her interests? That would show a nice, personal touch."

"Who is going to take the time to pick out all of these individual gifts?" inquired Vance Winkle. "It takes me a day and a half to find something each year for my wife's birthday."

"Well, maybe Annabelle could do it," suggested Alex.

"Thanks a lot," said Annabelle.

"No, Annabelle's much too busy to do that," interjected the Chair.

"Well, then why don't we ask students to register for the gifts they'd like? I'm sure that if all of the firms did it, stores would be delighted to set up registries," suggested Heather. "That would take the guesswork out of choosing a gift."

"If all of the firms did it, then we wouldn't have a very unique idea, would we, Heather?" commented Lionel. "Anyway, if we sent individual gifts, the students would all be comparing what they got, and some would feel that others got better gifts."

"I think you're right," said Vance. "What if we give them a gift certificate at a store that meets their personal interests and let them pick out whatever they like? That would assure their getting something they want, and would eliminate the notion that some students got a more expensive gift than others."

"No, that's too crass," said Heather. "It's like giving them cash. And the amount we'd be giving them would not be very great. Besides, it would require them to go out and buy something, which would take time, which is something they don't have during exams."

"Good point about the amount of the gift, Heather. What if instead of giving everyone a chintzy individual gift, we pooled the money, bought one really neat gift, and raffled it off to a summer associate? Maybe we could make it a trip to the Bahamas, over semester break," suggested Vance.

"Well, that's an interesting idea, in theory, Vance. All of the students would love it, at least until the drawing was held and they discovered that they hadn't won, but that all of their classmates were getting chintzy, individual gifts from our competitors. Then they'd all be moping."

"You're right, Annabelle. What's wrong with the sweatshirts that we had made with the Firm name on it, or the tote bags that we give them during the summer? We could have more of those made up and sent out to the students," suggested Alex.

"Those are dorky, Alex."

"What's dorky?"

"Anyone who doesn't know what dorky is is dorky. Can you imagine yourself as a law student wearing a sweatshirt with our Firm name on it around the law school? What a fashion statement!" said Heather.

"Yes, I suppose. But I do like the idea of giving a gift that has a certain longevity to it. I mean, the gift baskets we've sent are consumed in a week, and there's nothing left. As long as we're going to go through the trouble and expense of buying a gift, it would be nice to keep our name in front of them longer," said Alex.

"Do you have anything in mind, Alex?"

"Well, several of our clients send a fruit of the month, or a cheese of the month, or a wine, or even a mustard of the month."

"A mustard of the month?"

"Yes, the Mount Horeb Mustard Museum (www. mustard-museum.com; 1-800-438-6878), which was founded by a lawyer, Barry Levenson, who has agreed to give the author and the publisher of this book some free mustard if we mention him in this book, sends out great boxes of mustard."

"I think mustard is too creative for us (but it would be a very good idea for the readers of a satirical book about law firms), and those fruit or wine or cheese of the month deals are too expensive for us."

"Maybe we should do something tasteful," suggested Alex.

"I'm leaning strongly against it, but what did you have in mind?" asked Lionel.

"I'm thinking that maybe we should make a contribution to a charity in the names of our summer associates, and have the charity send an acknowledgment to each of them in thanks."

"Too tasteful. Besides, our summer associates want something for *them*, not for charity, so that will never fly."

"Maybe we should bake some goodies and send them to the students. That would be personal, and cheap," suggested Vance.

"Who are we going to get to do the baking?" asked Heather.

"Don't look at me," said Annabelle. "I don't cook, or do windows."

"Wait a minute," said Alex. "I think I've got the perfect idea. It's fun, it will get our name in front of them for a long time, and it's cheap."

"We're all ears," said the Chair.

"Why don't we give each one of them one of our thinking caps?"

"Brilliant," said the Chair. "Everybody loves them."

"See, I told you these thinking caps would produce new ideas. You just have to give them a little time."

Does Anyone Have a Match?

Distressed by the high incidence of turnover in its associate ranks, the firm of Fairweather, Winters & Sommers turned for advice to its longtime consultant, Harvey Tellum of Tellum, Whathey, Noh. Set forth below is TWN's analyis of the problem and its recommended course of action.

At your request, we have reviewed your statistics with regard to associate turnover. We can best summarize our reaction to what we found as "oh my god." Though it is true that you are not alone among large law firms in facing a turnover problem, we think that we should point out that while the average turnover period for associates in a large law firm is approximately four years, your associate class turns over as frequently as tables at an expensive New York restaurant. In fact, we recommend that you consider seatings for your associates.

There are two possible reasons why you may be experiencing the turnover that you have. The first is that you may be bringing in the wrong associates to begin with. The second is that while you have brought in the right associates, the environment within the Firm is such that those associates either fail or are driven away. Of course, the solution to the problem would differ depending on which cause you need to address.

Let's assume that the cause of failure or turnover is the environment of the Firm. To alter this, you would need to change the basic culture of the Firm. This likely would involve all of your partners going through an intense period of psychoanalysis, in the slim hope that this might radically change their personalities. Once psychoanalysis was completed and the partnership took on more humanoid characteristics, you could begin the job of melding the Firm into a more hospitable environment for your lawyers. Given the cost of this process, the length of time that it would consume, and the unlikelihood of its ultimate success, we recommend assuming that the cause of associate failure and turnover is your having brought in the wrong group of associates to the Firm to begin with.

Working on this assumption, we interviewed a group of twenty partners who have been involved in your recruitment efforts. We began by asking them what they were looking for in candidates, to predict who might be successful at the Firm. The responses we received fell into a pattern that led us to conclude that each of your partners regarded him- or herself as the ideal profile for candidates who would succeed. This propensity was perhaps demonstrated most starkly by Oscar Winters, just returned from the Great Barrier Reef and bearing a wicked sunburn on his pate, who allowed in our interview with him that in his experience, bald scuba divers made the very best lawyers at the Firm. We recommend that your lawyers be encouraged to adopt more flexible standards.

We next explored with your lawyers the method by which they sought to ascertain the qualifications of the candidates that they interviewed. On the positive side, it turns out that there was a high degree of consensus among your partners as to how to do this. On the somewhat less positive side, they were wrong. The most frequent penetrating questions your partners put to the law students they interviewed were the following:

1. Where do you see yourself in five years?
2. What is your weakest characteristic?
3. Why do you want to be a lawyer?
4. What can I tell you about the Firm?
5. Where do you see yourself ten years from now?
6. What is your strongest characteristic?
7. What was your favorite law school course?
8. Where do you see yourself in seven and a half years?

When asked why they asked these particular questions of law students, your partners replied that they did so because those were the questions they had been asked when they were in law school. Asked what they thought of those questions when they were asked them in law school, their answers could be summed up as follows: really stupid. When we inquired as to why they continued to ask questions they thought were really stupid, your partners replied with silence.

To get a better idea of how your partners were interviewing law students, we taped a dozen interviews. In reviewing the tapes, we noticed the following:

1. Your partners spoke during approximately 85% of the interview time. (They reported that they were very impressed with the interviewees, apparently because they had been listening to themselves talk.)

2. Your partners invited questions from the interviewee early in the interview. Since every interviewee has memorized twenty questions, your partners were put in the position of becoming the interviewee.

3. Your partners responded to concerns about the Firm's reputation as a sweatshop with a devastating 20-minute rebuttal, thus confirming by virtue of the length of the reply that your reputation is well deserved.

4. Your partners sold the Firm to law students on the basis of its "collegial atmosphere," the early responsibility given to associates, the high quality of your legal work, the excellence of your clients, and the fine training that associates receive. The video camera focused on the students during these replies detected that their eyes had glazed over from listening to the same things they'd heard from every firm with which they'd interviewed, from New York City to Topeka, KS, and that several students almost fell off of their chairs.

Ordinarily, TWN would recommend interviewer training to help your interviewers better identify appropriate candidates for the Firm. However, given the level of incompetence exhibited by your partners, we have concluded that trying to train them would be only slightly less difficult than changing the culture of the Firm. Instead, we have devised a simple test (set forth below) for the Firm to administer to prospective new associates to determine their suitability for practice at the Firm.

Simple Test for Prospective New Associates

Thank you for applying to the firm of Fairweather, Winters & Sommers. While other firms go through a laborious interview procedure that consumes enormous amounts of law students' and firm time, our firm finds that we can pretty-well predict who will succeed just as well through this little test. We will inform you of the test results within two weeks. Good luck.

1. I plan to work ...
    a. as much as I feel like.
    b. just enough to get by.
    c. 9-5.
    d. pretty darn hard.
    e. my ass off.
2. My position on ethical issues is ...
    a. holier than Thou.
    b. just as holy as Thou.
    c. totally independent of Thou.
    d. dependent on the context of the situation.
    e. governed by which position would benefit the
        Firm and its clients.
3. How much money I make ...
    a. means very little to me.
    b. is not that important, as long as I can get by.
    c. is important, but only one of many different factors.
    d. is not that important, as long as I'm wealthy.
    e. governs my *weltanschauung*.
4. High quality legal work ...
    a. is grossly overrated.
    b. seems like a pretty good idea.
    c. will unfortunately be necessary to the Firm's
        economic success.
    d. is something to strive for.
    e. is a *sine qua non* to real happiness and fulfillment.

5. Please write an essay on the topic: Why Fairweather, Winters & Sommers is the only firm for me and I'll just die if I don't get an offer. (Use as many extra sheets as necessary. We suggest at least six extra sheets, if you're really serious about getting this job.)

We at TWN believe that using the above simple test should allow you to decrease markedly the number of failures among associates at the Firm. For an additional fee, we will provide you with the correct answers to the questions.

Diverse Problems

The Fairweather, Winters & Sommers Long-Range Planning Committee was crocheting its collective brows, struggling with yet another thorny issue dropped in its collective lap by the Executive Committee.

"It's a problem," said Otto Flack, the Chair.

"Sure is, a *big* problem," added Sheldon Horwitz.

"Has been, for a long time," offered Helen Lasar.

"Getting to be even more serious," said Herb Gander.

"I think it's one of the bigger problems we have right now, as a firm," said James Freeport.

"I'm not sure I'd go that far, James. After all, we've got an awful lot of problems to choose among," said Otto.

"I only said, one of the bigger problems, not the biggest."

"Oh yes, definitely one of the bigger, you're right there, Jim."

"I might say it's the biggest," said Sheldon.

"You mean, you think it's bigger than our revenue problem?"

"That's a big one, too, Helen. But this may be bigger. What do you think, Jim?"

"Why does it matter whether it's the biggest, the second biggest, or the eighth biggest, Sheldon? We all agree it's big, don't we?"

"Oh, I think it makes a big difference how big it is, Jim. The eighth biggest problem might only be, say, a fourth or a fifth as big as the first biggest, and one of the problems we have, being blessed, as we are, with a bountiful number of big problems, is prioritizing them. We can't tackle every big problem we have all at once. We just don't have the resources for that."

"Well, whether or not it's the biggest problem, Sheldon, the Executive Committee has asked us to tackle it, so I think that makes it a big enough problem for me. I'm going to have to rule that any more discussion of the relative bigness of the problem is out of order," said Otto. "Now, I think we might want to begin by recalling a little Firm history, to set this problem into its current perspective."

"Ooh, good idea, Otto. Could I do that? Could I, please?" asked Sheldon.

"Fine, just go ahead."

"In the beginning, we were founded by a bunch of white guys, whose main diversity was height. In fact, the Firm made it a policy, early on, not to discriminate on the basis of height, as demonstrated by the fact that the first six partners ranged from 5'6" (Stanley Fairweather) to 6'4" (Oscar Winters). After only thirty years, the Firm hired a Jewish guy (though, technically, we didn't realize Shawn O'Brien was Jewish when we hired him) and about ten years after that, our first lawyer of the female persuasion was heartily welcomed aboard."

"I'd say 'heartily welcomed aboard' is overstating it a bit, Sheldon," interrupted Helen.

"Poetic license, Helen. A fellow's got to be allowed a little poetic license in recounting Firm history. Anyway, as I was saying, after we heartily welcomed our first woman abroad..."

"That's 'aboard,' not 'abroad,' Sheldon."

"Sorry ... After that, the Firm has dedicated itself fully and tirelessly to the need to diversify and, just to prove it, has adopted the following statement of policy:

> Whereas, it has always been the policy of this Firm to welcome lawyers of all races, colors, creeds, sexes, nationalities and so forth, and
> Whereas, it is deemed desirable to formalize what has always been the policy of this Firm in order to attract

more law students into this place and to pacify
certain clients who want to know we're dead
serious about this stuff,
NOW THEREFOR, it is hereby RESOLVED that we're
all really, really in favor of diversity, big time."

"And, yet, even with this policy, we have been unable to attract and retain a diverse group of lawyers? Hard to believe," mused James.

"We've gone even farther than the policy, though," said Sheldon.

"What else have we done?"

"Well, last year the Firm went out and hired a fulltime Director of Diversity Efforts to coordinate and marshal our firm's diversity efforts."

"That should certainly show that we're serious. Who did we hire?" asked James.

"A highly qualified individual, H.G. (Biff) Worthington III."

"I don't believe it. We hired a WASP male with numbers as our Director of Diversity Efforts? How did we manage to do that?" asked Helen.

"Well, it was quite easy, really. Biff was a college roommate of Oscar Winters' son, Randolph, at Princeton, and Biff had fallen on some hard times, so we decided to give him a break."

"Nice of us. What was his background in diversity?"

"Well, he didn't have what you would call a strong diversity background. But he's a big New York Knicks fan, and they have a lot of diverse players, so we figured that he was pretty committed to the concept."

"How's he been doing so far?" asked Helen.

"Well, he's taken a few missteps, but he's learning the ropes."

"What kind of missteps?"

"Well, he did introduce one of our African-American associates to a partner as 'one of our fine new Negroes.'"

"No, he didn't do that."

"I'm afraid he did. The associate corrected him, though, pointing out that minority lawyers prefer to be referred to 'as people of color.'"

"Well, at least he's been set straight now."

"Actually, he made another little faux pas after that."

"Okay, let's hear it."

"He introduced the same associate to another partner as 'one of our fine new colored lawyers.' I guess he thought he was shortening 'people of color.'"

"Sounds like a disaster. We've got to can old Biff before he does some irreparable damage."

"It may be a little bit late for that."

"You're kidding. What else did he do?"

"Well, he decided that we needed to take a more aggressive position in defending our diversity record, so he collected some statistics and defended our firm at one of our principal law schools by pointing out that over 20% of our lawyers are left-handed."

"If I can get us off of dear old Biff for a second, have we tried to analyze our results recruiting minorities? I don't understand why we haven't been more successful," said Otto.

"Yes, I think the problem is that minority students want to go to a place where they think they'll feel comfortable, and they're most comfortable where they see minority attorneys."

"So, what you're saying is, that in order to be successful in recruiting minorities, you have to have been successful in recruiting minorities, Sheldon?"

"Yes, that's pretty much right. And because there aren't all that many minority students who have the right credentials, it's a very tough market."

"Well, maybe we need to relax our standards in considering which minority candidates we're willing to hire," suggested James.

"Sounds sensible, but there's a problem with it."

"What's the problem?"

"Since we don't know what our standards are in the first place, it's tough to relax them," said Sheldon.

"Maybe we need to think outside the box. We do have a few minorities now. If we put them all into a minority department and hire new minority candidates into that department, perhaps they'd feel more comfortable," said Otto.

"Wonderful idea, Otto. Only we shouldn't call it a minority department, we should just call it what it would be known as anyway, 'the ghetto.'"

"I guess maybe this isn't such an easy problem to solve," said James.

"No, it's a *big* problem," said Helen.

"Maybe the biggest," said Sheldon.

"You're out of order," ruled Otto.

And the meeting adjourned.

Heaven Can Wait

"Where am I?" asked ace hiring partner Sherwood Corrigan, gazing around at the unfamiliar surroundings. Rows of smiling men and women, all about his age and all clad in white togas and sandals, were walking by him. Over the white togas everyone wore a gray, pin-striped vest. Looking down, Sherwood noticed that his own outfit matched that worn by the others.

"You have passed to the Great Beyond," two voices that seemed to come from above Sherwood said, simultaneously.

Glancing above him, Sherwood saw a two-headed figure, one head male and the other female. A long beard flowed together from both of their chins. "Who are you?" asked Sherwood, "And what do you mean by the Great Beyond? I'm not dead, am I? I'm too young to die."

"Relax," said the two-headed figure, in stereo. "You're not dead. But think, Sherwood, you've just experienced a major change in your life, haven't you?"

"What change in my life? I'm still married, live in a lovely split-level suburban house, drive a BMW, and have 2.3 lovely children, a dog named Butch, and a cat named Prosser. I still work my head off at the law firm and I still…"

"Hold it right there. Hasn't there been a change in your life at the firm?"

"Actually, there has. After eight years, I'm no longer the hiring partner."

"Aha! You've passed to the Great Beyond, to Hiring Partner Heaven, where all good hiring partners ascend after their stints with large law firms on earth."

"And you? Who are you?"

"Why the Lord, of course, the Lord of Recruitment."

"I notice that you have two heads…"

"You're very observant, Sherwood."

"And that you are both male and female, and appear to be of many races and nationalities, and seem to be sightless in a couple of your eyes and…"

"The Lord of Recruitment is a Diverse Lord of Recruitment. We practice what we preach up here, unlike the land where you came from."

"Don't you think that's a bit harsh? We did try our gosh darndest, and we managed to hire a few people of color."

"Tokenism."

"You *are* harsh."

"No, just truthful, Sherwood. That's another difference between here and the land from whence you came. Here we tell it like it is."

"And all the other people I see walking around here, are they former hiring partners from other firms?"

"Bingo."

"But they all look the same."

"And you wonder why the law students you recruited had such difficulty distinguishing you from the other firms?"

"But how did I get up here?"

"You were transported here in your sleep by me, the Lord of Recruitment."

"How did you know that I had retired?"

"Retired? Let's be honest, Sherwood, you didn't exactly retire. After eight years, you were eased out by the Executive Committee because you began to exhibit some of the aberrant behavior that many partners who have held the position of hiring partner too long display."

"Such as?"

"Such as asking your wife whether she has any questions for you about the firm, and preparing a family resume for your seven-year-old daughter, Amy. To answer your earlier question,

I found out about your retirement from the National Association for Law Placement."

"NALP? You mean the National Association for Law Placement has a direct line to heaven?"

"Of course they do. And they have complex rules about which dates we can bring you up here, and how long we can keep you, and what questions we can ask you, and..."

"So it's sort of like back home? You can't escape the NALP rules even in Hiring Partner Heaven?"

"'Fraid not. Heaven's not perfect, you know."

"How long will I be up here, and what will I do?"

"That depends. We run a sort of de-tox program up here in Hiring Partner Heaven. And since you've been hiring partner for eight years, it's likely to take quite a while to clean you out."

"Well, I still don't get it."

"Come with me, I'll show you around a little. Can you tell what we have going on in here?"

"Looks like an Executive Committee meeting."

"Very good, Sherwood. How could you tell?"

"Well, they're in a fancy board room, they're all men, and none of them appears to be listening to what any of the others are saying."

"Exactly. But now, watch. See, they're bringing in one of the hiring partners in her toga. Let's listen."

"Please sit down, Sally. I'm R. Langford Huxley III. My friends call me Hux. I'm Chair of the Executive Committee here in Hiring Partner Heaven."

"Nice to meet you, Hux."

"Ah, Sally, I said my *friends* call me Hux. You and I just met, so, if you don't mind, I'd appreciate your calling me Mr. Huxley III."

"Oh, of course, sorry, Mr. Huxley III."

"Uh, Sally, me and the rest of the EC called you in here to tell you how much we on the EC appreciate the fine work that you've done as hiring partner at our firm. We know that you didn't get thanked much back on earth, and that you put in hundreds of hours each year without any compensation for it, and that we second-guessed most of your decisions and complained about how you weren't getting the type of quality lawyers we used to get (by which we meant, people just like us), and that we sliced your budget in half and, well, I could go on and on, but I just wanted to say that you did one helluva job, Sally, and we on the EC appreciate it, big time, and so we've prepared this resolution, suitable for framing, that reads, 'In appreciation for a job well done, the EC awards Sally Freebish this certificate of recognition.' And, looky here, this has been signed by each and every one of us on the EC."

"C'mon, Sherwood, time to go. What did you think of that?"

"I guess it was nice. I mean, they recognized her. But it all seemed a bit stilted and artificial."

"Well, we're not miracle workers up here in Hiring Partner Heaven, Sherwood. We *are* dealing with an Executive Committee. And we've made progress. The first Executive Committee we had up here voted a certificate of appreciation by a vote of 5-4. At least we've got them in unanimous agreement now. Let's duck into this next room, here, where we've got a bunch of law students speaking to a group of hiring partners."

"And so, we law students have been thinking more about our decisions. We were all so impressed with you and your firms—and we liked each of you the best of all—that we've changed our minds and, instead of rejecting your offers, we would all like to accept all of your offers."

"What do you think of that, Sherwood?"

"It doesn't seem plausible to me. I mean, how could they all like us the best?"

"Well, you never seemed to question it when every law student who turned down your offer told you that you were their *second* choice, so why would you find it implausible when they all told you that they thought you were the best?"

"You make a good point, there, Lord of R. But what they tell us wouldn't be good news, even if it were true. My worst nightmares as hiring partner were always that every law student would accept our offers. If that ever happened, my partners would kill me. I'm getting out of here."

"Wait a minute, Sherwood. Stop trying to take that toga off, and come back here. You still haven't gotten to the rooms in Hiring Partner Heaven in which they teach you not to smile like an idiot all the time and where they wipe out some of the hackneyed phrases you've built into your vocabulary, such as "collegial," "cutting edge," "early responsibility," and "meritocracy." Sherwood, why are you clicking your heels?"

"There's no place like home, there's no place like home..."

Temporarily Out of Order

"We just can't seem to make our quota anymore," said Sherwood Corrigan, Chair of the Fairweather, Winters & Sommers Hiring Committee.

"I don't understand it, though," said Heather Regale. "The market is real tight now, so you'd think that hiring law students ought to be like shooting fish in a barrel."

"You might think that, but unfortunately it's not true," noted Alex Pouts. "When the market gets tight, historically our acceptance percentages go down."

"But that makes no sense," moaned Lionel Hartz.

"Actually, it does," argued Alex.

"How so?" asked Vance Winkle.

"Well, follow me here, if you will," suggested Alex.

"We'll sure as heck try," offered Heather. "Lead us."

"Okay. When the market gets tight, all firms are hiring fewer students."

"Exactly my point," said Lionel. "If everyone's hiring fewer students, the competition ought to be less, and so it ought to be easier to hire."

"In theory," admitted Alex.

"Well, why isn't it in practice, as well as theory?" asked Heather.

"Simple. Every firm has it figured out the same way we just described it. So everyone thinks that it will be easy to hire in this market. That means that everyone also figures that this should present a great opportunity for them to upgrade the quality of the students they are hiring."

"But according to the laws of supply and demand, that ought to be true, shouldn't it?" asked Lionel.

"Sure, but it doesn't work."

"And why not?" asked Heather.

"Because everyone's doing the same thing. For example, let's suppose that in a strong market a group of law firms is looking for 100 students in the top 50% of their law school class. In a weak market, those same firms may be looking for 70 students in the top 25% of the law school class. Do the math."

"So that's going to make it more, rather than less competitive," announced Lionel.

"Bingo," said Alex.

"Great, Alex," said Rex Gladhand. "But now that we've analyzed the problem, what do we do about getting the number of lawyers that we need?"

"Well, it seems to me that we've got to look for the lawyers in a different, less competitive place," suggested Alex.

"You mean in the bottom half of the class?" asked Heather.

"No, I don't mean the bottom half of the class, though it wouldn't hurt us to reexamine the standards we apply at some schools. We might ask ourselves, for example, why laterals we hire from a school can do quite spectacularly at our firm if they finished in the top half of the class at a certain law school, but we insist on hiring new associates only from the top quarter of the class of the same school."

"Well, if you're not suggesting that we hire lower in the class, Alex, what do you mean?"

"I mean that we should look outside the traditional sources we've tapped."

"Are you suggesting that we should be interviewing at law schools where we haven't recruited before?"

"Well, that certainly would be one possibility," said Alex.

"But we haven't recruited at those schools before because we thought they wouldn't be a very likely source of talent for us," noted Heather, "either because the school was in another part of the country and so its students weren't particularly interested in our city, or because the school was located near us but wasn't very good. So what makes you think all of a sudden that these schools would become good sources of new associates for us?"

"Right. I wasn't actually thinking of going to other schools."

"Okay, if you weren't thinking of going lower in the class or to different schools, I give up, what other source were you thinking of?"

"I was thinking of temporary associates."

"These days it seems as if *all* our associates were temporary associates; we hire them, they come temporarily, and then they take off, usually just as we're beginning to make a profit on them," said Lionel.

"No, I mean associates the Firm hires with the intention that they'll just be with us for a limited period of time, for example, to staff a major case."

"That seems like a terrible idea to me, Alex. How are we going to control the quality of the work they do for us?"

"Same way we control the quality of the work our regular associates do for us, by supervising them."

"But won't it create ethical problems if these people come and go willy-nilly and have access to our clients' confidential information?"

"Of course we'd have to watch that, but we have mechanisms in place now to check for potential conflicts in the laterals we hire. We'd simply apply the same methods to avoid conflicts with temporary associates."

"I'd be concerned about our ability to get quality attorneys as temps," said Heather. "Won't we just get people who couldn't get a job at a good firm?"

"No, the resumes of some of the temporary associates I've seen are pretty stellar. Many of them have just made the decision that they don't want to work the crazy hours we require of our so-called permanent associates."

"Still, hiring attorneys on a case-by-case basis seems like more trouble than it's worth, unless there are some pretty big advantages," opined Rex.

"Well, there certainly are some advantages," replied Alex.

"Such as?"

"Well, for one thing, we won't have to pay them the same outlandish salaries we pay our new associates."

"That's good."

"And we won't have the steep recruitment costs we incur in attracting our new associates."

"True."

"It would give us some flexibility, too, since it allows us to avoid the fixed overhead that we undertake when we hire regular associates."

"That sounds like a good thing."

"And because these temporary attorneys are independent contractors, we don't have to pay benefits, which will save us a bundle."

"Yes, benefits probably add 50% or so to the salaries that we pay."

"Don't forget, too, that we'll save all the time we take for performance reviews of regular associates, and we won't have to agonize over whether to fire them."

"I hadn't thought of that."

"And, of course, we won't have to worry about partnership decisions with temporary associates."

"No, I guess not."

"Temporary associates won't be insisting on mentors, either, or on extensive training programs or on creating an associates committees."

"Wait a minute, Alex. Unless I'm missing something here," said Heather, "it seems to me that by hiring temporary associates we avoid pretty much every problem we have with our regular associates, and we save a hell of a lot of money in the process."

"That would appear to be the case."
"I have only one question then?"
"What's that, Heather?"
"Can we hire temporary partners?"

Self-Fulfilling Prophecies

Ace hiring partner Sherwood Corrigan was invited to address his partners recently on the subject of why associates are leaving large law firms. Here is an unedited transcript of a portion of Sherwood's remarks.

Fellow partners, and you lady partners, too [VERY MILD LAUGHTER, COMING PRIMARILY FROM THE SPEAKER], it is an honor and a privilege to address you today (as it would be most any day). Having been entrusted with the yoke of hiring partner for what seems like about the past eighty-three years, I have had opportunity to reflect on the people we are bringing in, and why many of them appear (outwardly, at least) not to be the happy little clams that we partners think they damn well ought to be.

My friends, I think we need to rewind the tape to back before law school even begins and ask who these students are that wind up in those hallowed halls. By and large, law students are the people who can't stand the sight of blood (and therefore opt out of medical school) and who do not see themselves as sufficiently greedy to plunge into the business school arena. In my observation, relatively few of these students enter with a strong sense that law school is where they want to be, that a career at the bar is their dream. They are a body of well-schooled, high-achieving liberal arts majors, who fancy themselves "big picture" people. Many of them are interesting folks, the type you might like to have over to dinner to talk about a wide range of topics. Instead of being attracted by what law school has to offer, many of them are there because they perceive that going to law school may, somehow, "maximize their options."

Thus, with this decision to go to law school begins what I call the "option-maximization syndrome." These English and political science and history majors take the law boards and are thrilled at how well they do (I'd tell you their scores, but the law school testing service changes the scoring system so often that few of you would know what I meant, anyway), thus confirming in their minds that their decision to head to law school was a brilliant one. Which law school to choose? Well, if maximizing your options is a primary reason for going to law school, it makes good sense to further maximize those options by going to the best, most prestigious law school that will have you.

Once these innocents hit the halls of the prestigious law schools around the country, they notice that the students in the two classes above them seem to have little interest in law school. In fact, many of them spend precious little time around the place. Soon our first year students discover the reason: these upper class students are being wined and dined by some of the fanciest law firms around the country. Firm names begin floating around the school, most of them sounding indistinguishable from one another. Then comes the chatter and the scuttlebutt. Such and such a law firm is tops. It's the largest, or its partners make the most money, or it's the "coolest" — students are dying to get in there. So our student thinks, "Such & Such must be the place for me. After all, it is so prestigious that it's bound to maximize my options. Once I've worked there, I can go anywhere."

In the shuffle, a few little things get lost. True, our student is from Dubuque, Iowa and has never set foot in a city of more than 500,000 people before going to law school, and Such & Such is located in New York, or L.A., or Chicago. True, the lawyers at Such & Such work 18 hours a day, and our student has many outside interests. Little hitches like that, though, are swept away in the drive to maximize options.

Other pressures conspire to push the student in the same direction. The placement office at the law school touts large law firms. They are the ones that come to campus, they hire the largest number of students, and the placement director is under great pressure to get her students placed. What will *U.S. News & World Report* think if the percentage of students placed drops? Worse, what will the dean think? The dean wants students in those Such & Such-type firms, too. Their prestige reflects well on the school, and Such & Such lawyers donate generously to their alma mater.

Then, too, there's the peer pressure generated by classmates, all of them after the same "plum" firms. And the subtle hints of professors and adjunct professors, who drop the names of those firms in their classes. It's a mighty strong student who bucks this current. Indeed, ironically, the student strong enough to buck that current just might be the one most likely to succeed at a large law firm.

Finally, perhaps the greatest pressure pushing students in our direction (let's face it, we're Such & Such) is debt. Many of these students are staring at loans of close to six figures when they emerge from law school. Not surprisingly, there's a lot of interest in taking the highest paying job they can find in order to reduce that debt as quickly as possible.

Preconditioned by all of these forces to choose firms like ours, the students are then fed into the recruitment whirlwind. Wined and dined by our firms in the fall, and then again in the summer, many of these students think that this is a taste of what life will be like once they arrive. Even if they say that they know that this will not be the case, they don't appreciate just how much this will not be the case.

And though they seem sophisticated, and all sorts of information is available to them from the legal press, websites and elsewhere, these students haven't the foggiest idea how a law firm is run, what issues firms like ours face, how every decision that is made by a firm affects almost every other decision that needs to be made. It's hardly surprising that they haven't any idea about these things. If we're honest with ourselves, few of us partners have much of an idea how the Firm runs, either.

These students have succeeded all their lives. Many of them

think they've worked hard to do so, and they have. But they have no idea of the difference between working hard in school, where you can largely determine your schedule, and working hard at a firm, where you are largely subject to the whims of any client or partner you are working for. When they find out the difference, they generally don't like it very much.

So we attract people who went to law school not particularly intent on practicing law in the first place, coming to us based on unrealistic expectations that we are, in part, responsible for creating, to maximize their options and repay their debt, with no real intention of staying for the long haul. In part, their expectation of not staying for the long haul is based upon the reality of seeing that, even if they wanted to, the chances are greatly against them becoming a partner. This contributes to a vicious cycle in which students enter our firm with an employee attitude and are greeted by partners who resent the high salaries being paid to these new associates and who, loaded with pressures of all kinds ourselves, are unwilling to invest the time to establish relationships and to train people we expect will be with us only a short time. That contributes to making the associates' expectations a self-fulfilling prophecy.

Unfortunately, many of the associates who might well make it to partner look around at the pressures they see us under, and conclude that this is not what they want to do when they grow up. They see the "big picture" at our firm and it's not quite the "big picture" they saw as liberal arts undergrads. They don't want to be us when they grow up.

Now that I've explained the problem, as I see it, it should be a relatively simple thing for you to fix it. Fortunately, I only hire them, it's up to somebody else to retain them. As Tom Lehrer used to say in his song about Werner von Braun, the famous German-born, U.S. rocket scientist, "Vunce ze rocket goes up, who cares vere it comes down. Zats not my department, said Werner von Braun."

[AUDIBLE WEEPING FROM AROUND THE HALL]

The Last Word

Every aspect of the practice of law has changed dramatically since I began to practice umpty-ump years ago. Well, almost every aspect. The one that's changed the least—damn little, in fact—is how we recruit attorneys. Now that's probably a hint, right there, that something's amiss.

When you get right down to it, and that's pretty much where I like to get, there are only two aspects to recruiting— identifying the right folks to hire and convincing them to come to the Firm. Now here's how we identify the right people to hire — we cede the job to law professors, most of whom are folks that haven't practiced law a day in their life and who make their judgment based on a student's performance in a setting that is pretty-near irrelevant to practicing law. Why do we do that? I suppose because we must think it's too tough to figure out ourselves who we should hire.

Now me, I don't think it's so tough. Here's how I'd hire people: I'd figure that most of the top students at good law schools are plenty smart enough to practice with us. (Though it's devastating for most of my partners to admit this, the vast majority of what we do is not rocket science.) I'd invite law students over to a party at my house and, because I like to cook, I'd be in the kitchen cutting things up. Now some of the students would stand there watching me. Others would wander off into the living room, where other folks were congregating. Still others might ask me half-heartedly whether I could use some help. And a small group would pick up the extra knife on the counter and start slicing tomatoes. Give me those tomato slicers, and I'll form one hell of a good law firm.

And as to attracting them to the Firm, I'd stop doing it by pretending we're who we aren't. If they don't like us now, warts and all, they're not going to like us that way in a couple of years, either.

Stanley J. Fairweather

Associates

One Size Fits All

At the same time the Fairweather, Winters & Sommers Hiring Committee was puzzling over how to attract additional bodies to the Firm, another committee was charged with disposing of excess bodies already at the Firm. As a result of the Firm's strict rules regarding confidentiality of committee proceedings, the two committees were blissfully unaware of each other's efforts.

"CARE will come to order," announced Chair Manny Candoo.

"Wait a minute, how can we still be called CARE? We're meeting to decide how to fire a bunch of associates," said Harriet Akers. "CARE stands for Committee on Associate Retention and Evaluation."

"Used to," said the Chair.

"What do you mean 'used to'?"

"Well, the committee's name has been changed, but we're still CARE. It now stands for the Committee on Associate Redeployment and Elimination. And we're not firing anybody."

"That's right," said Lance Byte, "we're downsizing."

"No, downsizing sounds too negative, so what we've decided to do, instead, is to rightsize," corrected the Chair. "Now our first issue is how to go about rightsizing."

"What do you mean? We decide how many is the right size and we keep firing until we hit that number," offered Lance.

"That's obvious," said David Alms, "but we need to decide whom to fire."

"Isn't that pretty simple: we go down the list of associates and get rid of the weakest ones," said Harriet.

"No, that could present some serious problems. Our weakest associates might have trouble finding new positions. If we have a lot of attorneys out in the market without positions, that's going to leak out to the press and come back to haunt us in our recruitment efforts," said David. "And anyway, firing weak associates would be inconsistent with the press release that we want to put out, saying that these layoffs were not because of poor performance by associates, but were due to the general economy."

"So if we say that in our press release, why can't we just get rid of the weakest performers, since nobody else will think they're the weakest if our press release says we're laying people off for economic reasons?" asked Harriet.

"C'mon now, Harriet, you know that nobody is going to actually believe our press release," Otto Flack pointed out.

"So if nobody is going to believe our press release, why are we going to base our decision on what it says?" asked Harriet.

"Well, we certainly don't want to get the reputation of putting out misleading press releases, do we?" said Flack.

"You've got a point there," chimed Patrick Conshenz.

"What are we going to tell firms that call us to ask for references about the lawyers we've rightsized out of jobs?"

"Don't we just give the associate's name, rank, and serial number? Otherwise can't we get into big trouble?" asked Harriet.

"No, we just tell our clients to do that. We ignore our own advice. Whoever happens to answer the phone says pretty much anything that he or she wants to say about lawyers who have left."

"Can't we change that, tell our partners what they should say in giving references?"

"We can tell our partners anything, but when's the last time our partners listened to anything we told them?"

"Good point. But what if we just have anybody who gets a call refer it to a central source?"

"Right, Harriet. And if you believe that's really going to happen, I have a couple really nice bridges I'd like to sell you."

"Uh, getting back to the question at hand, I think we ought to identify our strongest associates and fire them," suggested Conshenz.

"You must be out of your mind, Pat. Why in the world would we get rid of our best associates?"

"There are two reasons that I would have thought were rather self-evident, but as they weren't evident to at least one self, I guess I'll spell them out. First, these being our strongest associates, they should have no problem finding another position, thus avoiding the problems discussed earlier about having riff-raff from our firm floating around the market. And second, since our history clearly demonstrates that our strongest associates inevitably leave our firm early in their careers in any case, we lose nothing by being proactive and inviting them to do so."

"Maybe we should do the firing, I mean rightsizing, by department," suggested the Chair. "Some of our departments are a lot less profitable or less busy than others; we could get rid of associates in those departments."

"No, that's not a good idea. We don't want to give associates the impression that their success at the Firm is dependent on which department they happen to work in," said Lance.

"But their success at the Firm *is* dependent on which department they work in."

"Of course it is, but we don't want to give them that impression. Anyway, we couldn't do that to our partners in those departments," argued Lance.

"Why not? If those partners' work is down, and they don't really need the number of associates they have, what's the problem in asking them to get rid of some of their associates?"

"Have you no heart? Our partners' self-esteem is intimately tied up with how many associates they have working for them. If you take away some of their associates just because the department's work load doesn't require them, our entire real estate section is going to be moping around the place. And you know what a moping real estate department is like."

"You're right, Lance, I don't know what I could have been thinking about. We accountants rely on LIFO quite a bit. Maybe we should use that approach with our associates; last in, first out."

"No, the last to come in are our cheapest associates. The Firm would save a lot more money if we fired some of those who've been around longer," argued Otto.

"Okay, then how about FIFO?"

"No, I don't think a mechanical method is going to work, whether it's LIFO, FIFO, or MIFO," opined Harriet.

"What's MIFO?"

"Middle in, first out. What if we just gave each department a quota and left it up to them who to fire?" suggested Harriet.

"No, we're all one firm; we don't want to be creating divisions," said the Chair.

"We've already got divisions, Manny. That's what departments are: divisions."

"I think it would be fairer if we did it more randomly," suggested David. "What if we just have associates draw lots."

"Oh, that's humane and sensible, David. Why don't we just do it by height?" asked Harriet.

"Actually, I hadn't thought about doing it by height, Harriet. Would we get rid of the tallest or the shortest? And we'd have to make sure that height isn't a protected class. I could have some research done on it."

"I was just kidding, David. But maybe we're not thinking creatively enough. Maybe we need to think outside the box."

"What box?"

"Maybe we should call this a 'leave of absence,' and sell it to law students as a recruitment tool," suggested Otto.

"How is this a leave of absence? We're firing them," asked Harriet.

"Well, I suppose we'd have to describe it as an involuntary, indefinite leave of absence without pay, to be absolutely candid," Otto conceded.

"Any law student who falls for that description is somebody we wouldn't want to hire, in any case," said Lance. "But there may be another approach. This whole thing is driven by cost, right? So what if we just ask the associates to take a cut in pay, to make a salary concession?"

"Yes, but there still wouldn't be enough work. Associates would probably only be averaging about 1750 billable hours per year."

"Wait a minute, Otto, it was only a few years ago when we thought that 1750 wasn't such a bad number to shoot for. So, would it really be so bad if lawyers worked that number of hours for a reduced wage?"

"Trouble is, we'll get busy again in a few months," said Manny, "and then they'll have gotten used to working a reasonable number of hours and developing a lifestyle that allows for some time with their families and for their other interests, and then we're going to have a hell of a time getting them to go back to working ridiculous hours just to make more money they don't have time to enjoy anyway."

"Yeah, you're right, Manny, that would be terrible. We can't go back to having a reasonable billable hours requirement."

"I've got an idea. Why don't we just leave it up to the associates to determine who's dismissed and who survives?" suggested Patrick.

"You mean just have them vote their fellow associates off the island?"

"Sure. Maybe we could even get some TV network interested in carrying the show. That would help us with the economic problems that got us into this mess in the first place."

Justice Beyond

Fairweather, Winters & Sommers associate Tom Wisham, a Phi Beta Kappa in English as an undergraduate, dreamt of the day when he would no longer have to toil at the law, a profession he'd entered because he couldn't stand the sight of blood. Inspired by the legal writing instructor the Firm had brought in to help associates improve their writing skills, Tom has begun a novel about lawyers in space, which he hopes will one day allow him to escape the gravity of the law. Tom's novel begins as follows:

To the nude earthling eye, Iota IV is the barest speck, a freckle on the upper lip of the Tuna Nebula. Mythology tells us the Tuna Nebula was spawned by a big splash in the Fisherman's Galaxy, which threw the great tuna off its hook and washed it away to form its own nebula some 14 billion years ago, give or take a decade. Iota IV is believed to be the very spot at which the hook pierced the tuna's lip.

Though all but a few earthlings remain ignorant of Iota IV's wonders, residents of nearby stars and planets regard Iota IV as a paradise. Tourism is among its major industries. Visitors travel light years to vacation on Iota IV, especially when the intergalactic transportation companies run supersaver or kids-fly-free promos.

What attracts the tourists? For one thing, the lovely sunsets. The forty-two suns of Iota IV set almost continuously, sparing photographers the agony of missing the perfect shot. Double, triple, and sometimes even quadruple sunsets on Iota IV offer experiences that visitors never forget.

Another tourist attraction is the variety of gases. Traveling from one part of the planet to another, visitors can experience the inner and outer delights of Iota IV's gases. Their varied colors and shapes, constantly changing, produce a kaleidoscope of beauty to the eye; their scents and effects create states of mind unknown on other planets. Inhale the orange gas of Gary, Iota IV and all inhabitants of the planet seem temporarily to become rutabagas, an occurrence the more unusual because no natural rutabaga grows within four light years and three light months of Iota IV.

Iota IV is a safe place. There are the iggonauts, to be sure. But every place has its iggonauts, its antisocials, its evilwreakers. The iggonauts, at least, keep pretty much to themselves. The two reported instances of iggonauts straying from their home city of Zyck, Iota IV, though disturbing if true, are generally considered aberrations. Some doubt that they happened at all.

Death is unknown on Iota IV. That is not to say that nobody dies. But nobody knows that anybody dies. Something in the atmosphere of Iota IV or the minds of Iotaians makes people forget that people who disappear ever lived.

In his room on Iota IV, earthling lawyer Kevin Hogue was thinking about death. He wondered who back home might have "passed on," tangoed his last tango. Now that he thought about it, the Iota IV attitude toward the dead was not so very different from the policy back at his law firm, the earth branch of Hotchkiss & Raxo, P.C. Who among the former partners was still remembered? Only R. Franklin Hotchkiss.

It was Fritz Hotchkiss – those assuming a false familiarity with him betrayed themselves by calling him Frank – who, even in the days before government was Government, had had the foresight to recognize that one day government would be Government. It was governments, Fritz realized, that would one day have the wealth, not individuals. It was governments, not individuals, that would provide the services. It was governments, not individuals, that would be the center of the real action and excitement.

Now these observations may no longer seem singular in their insightfulness. But it is the nature of genius to make observations that history finds obvious. And Fritz took his observations a step further. If government was to assume the importance he saw for it, government would need a friend. Fritz could use a friend himself, he thought. Fritz would become government's friend.

Not, of course, overnight. There were many willing to befriend power. Fritz's unique quality was that he demanded nothing in return—no fees, no credit, no publicity, no thanks, no kid glove treatment—nothing. For Fritz, it was enough at first just to be there. The rest, he knew, would come with time.

Government needed good friends, Fritz knew, the type who could keep their mouths shut. Government required secrets, many secrets. And the bigger the government, the bigger the secrets it required. The people might have a right to know, but not very much. Fritz was a very good friend.

Over the years, then, H & R, P.C. became the friend of government, first under Fritz Hotchkiss' steady guidance, and then under the guidance of his hand-picked successor, the brilliant Tal Raxo. Gradually, gracefully, Tal had replaced Fritz as the firm's contact to government. The nature of Tal's work was so confidential that even within the firm it was disguised from those who didn't need to know by the use of phony client names on newly-opened files, and it was protected in other ways, even from those who did need to know. And as it learned more and more of government's secrets, H & R, P.C. became more and more indispensable, both because of how effective it proved on the inside and because of the importance of keeping it there.

Kevin Hogue's mind wandered back to the day that Tal Raxo had assigned him the case that brought him here to Iota IV. The task had seemed so routine. An H & R client, Ms. Tunder-Zolt, was planning to make an investment in a business on Iota

IV, a sizeable investment, to be sure—six trillion U.S. dollars. A Business—that was the name of the company in which Ms. Tunder-Zolt was about to invest—was in the leisure industry. A Business dealt with minds. It made games that were played entirely in the mind: no boards, no instruments, nothing to touch with the hands. This was just as well, since the residents of Iota IV had neither hands nor arms.

Raxo had told Hogue that the H & R team was to give A Business the once-over, to do what was known on earth as a corporate check: look over the books, talk to the key officers, in short, make sure that everything at the company was kosher before their client plunked down her six tril. Hogue chuckled as he thought about the conversation he'd had with Tal Raxo about staffing the case. He'd told Tal that he needed five lawyers to do the job.

"Can't spare 'em," said Tal.

"Well, I've got two paralegals," Kevin had said.

"Loses to three of a kind," said Tal, and he chuckled.

Kevin had chuckled, too. He hadn't thought Tal's remark particularly clever, but he had long since learned that when Tal Raxo chuckled, you chuckled. Non-chucklers didn't last long around H & R. Kevin chuckled as he thought about the incident.

Kevin glanced up and caught sight of the bars on the window of his room on Iota IV. He stopped chuckling. Precious little to chuckle about, when you got right down to it. Kevin missed Gladiola, his wife, though he knew that she wouldn't miss him. Another Kevin would be tending to her now. She wouldn't know the difference.

Why hadn't anyone been sent to rescue them? Tal would have missed them by now. It had been eighteen earth years since they'd left on their corporate check and they'd not been able to send so much as a picture postcard home. Surely Raxo must suspect that something had gone awry.

Kevin shook his head. Tal would never in a million light years guess what had happened to them. A simple corporate

check, eh? Well, that's one thing about the practice of law: even the most routine matter has a way of becoming a big megillah. Who could have predicted that, in the course of looking at the books of A Business, Holly LeBlanc, a lowly paralegal, would come across documents that would expose the planned conquest of Earth? And, on top of it, run smack into some iggonauts. The odds against that, Kevin reckoned, must have been a zillion to one, maybe two zillion. But those weren't the odds Kevin was interested in right now. No, he was far more interested in the odds of another H & R team reaching them soon, before it was too late.

"Blast!" thought Kevin, "Blast!" Maybe Tal had already sent somebody to rescue them and the rescuers had gone astray or fallen prey to the same misfortune. "Is this why I went to law school?" Kevin asked himself, rhetorically. "To die a captive, unnoticed, on Iota IV?" But Tal Raxo would not let him down. No way.

To make the time pass more quickly, Kevin began to review in his mind the incredible sequence of events that had gotten him into his present predicament.

Note: Wisham had to drop the story temporarily at this point in order to close a real estate deal.

Hello Muddah, Hello Fadduh

I dont' get it, why isn't sending a plant enough?" asked David Alms, midway through a recent CARE meeting. "If the mother needs a little time to recuperate, fine, that's medical. But unless I don't recall my high school biology correctly—and it *has* been a few years—I don't see why we need to do anything for the father."

"David, sending a plant isn't exactly what associates mean when they talk about the firm being 'family friendly,'" said Harriet Akers.

"I'm family friendly, Harriet. I'm family friendly as hell, in fact. I've got absolutely no objection to any of our associates having just as many kids as they like. Just let them raise them on their own time, not ours."

"But it's important for parents to spend quality time with their kids, David," said Patrick Conshenz.

"Quality time? With what? For the first several months, the kid's a vegetable, anyway; it eats, sleeps, and craps, what else? I don't see why a nanny changing the kid's diaper isn't as much quality time as the parent doing it. In fact, recalling my time as the parent of an infant, I'd say that changing a diaper was about the lowest quality time I spent, from my standpoint."

"We are a firm that promotes family values, aren't we?" asked Lance Byte.

"Oh, get off of it, Lance. We're not running for public office here, we're trying to run a law firm for a profit, and this family leave isn't helping our bottom line. I still don't see why the mother needs more than a week or two to recover."

"You're on the wrong track, David. This is not a medical leave we're talking about. I mean, let's be honest, basically, we're doing this for recruitment purposes," said Harriet.

"Well, if we're doing it for recruitment purposes, why don't we go whole hog: let both parents stay on leave until the kid's in college?"

"I think that's going overboard, David. We just need to come up with a reasonable length of time, something fair and uniform. Now, I think that three months for the woman and two weeks for the man is probably a sensible period."

"I thought you said it should be uniform, Harriet. Three months and two weeks doesn't exactly sound uniform to me."

"Well, I think that a differential simply recognizes the reality that women today are generally the primary caregivers."

"You mean, this progressive firm is going to accept that sexist stereotype, Harriet? Are we suggesting that a man can spend all of the quality time he needs to with a baby in two weeks and it takes a female three months to do that? I'm very disappointed in you, and a little bit ashamed to be associated with such a firm."

"Maybe David has a point, Harriet," said Patrick. "Perhaps we should make the leave policy three months for both males and females."

"Well, I don't think that makes sense, Pat. We have trouble convincing men to take the one week that we allow them to take now."

"Why's that?"

"I think it's because they feel it won't be perceived well by the Firm. It will be taken as an indication that the associate isn't serious about his work."

"In that case, I think we should give our male associates six months leave," suggested David.

"And why would we do that?"

"It's a little bit like the story of the guy who goes into a dealership to buy a car. He describes exactly the car that he wants – the color, the model, the accessories, everything – and asks the dealer what the car will cost him. The dealer says that it will cost \$32,900. The guy says that that's ridiculous, another dealer a couple blocks away will sell the exact same car to him for \$29,700. The dealer asks the guy why he doesn't just buy the car from the other dealer, then. The guy tells him that, unfortunately, the other dealer doesn't have the car available now and can't get one. The dealer says, 'Oh, when I can't get this car, I sell it for \$27,500.'"

"I don't get the connection, David."

"If we know that male associates won't take even a week, let's offer them six months. It will show that we're in the very forefront of family friendliness, and it won't cost the Firm a thin dime."

"If our male associates aren't taking paternity leave, maybe we need to take another tack altogether," suggested Patrick.

"And what might that tack be?"

"Perhaps we need to *require* male associates to take paternity leave."

"Oh, that'd be a great message for our recruits, Pat. The Firm is so devoted to its work that it needs to compel its associates to take family leave. Maybe we should just set up a Firm adoption agency to put associates' kids up for adoption," said Harriet. "And I can just see the great press we'll get when the first male associate tries to avoid taking our required leave by denying that he is the father of his wife's child."

"Okay, so perhaps that's not such a good idea," admitted Patrick.

"I think that maybe we need to refine this whole policy a bit more," suggested David. "I'm not so sure that uniformity is the ticket."

"What kind of refinements are you thinking about, David?"

"Well, for one thing, I'm not sure that the male/female difference makes sense. Maybe the longer leave should be given to the principal caregiver, and we could allow the couple to designate that."

"But then what do we do with this situation? Assume that both mother and father are working. The father works for us, and the mother's firm allows her three months leave. Our male associate claims that he is the principal caregiver, and so they both get three months off."

"Well, I suppose that we'd have to monitor the situation; we couldn't just accept a couple's word as to who was the principal caregiver. We'd need reports filed weekly on burpings, feedings, changings, etc. And we might need to set up some surveillance equipment around the house, to make sure we're not getting ripped off."

"Excellent. What other types of refinements do you have in mind, David?"

"Well, I don't believe it's reasonable to assume that it takes the same amount of time to raise a second or a third child as it does to raise a first child, so I think we should recognize that in the length of time the Firm offers."

"Good idea, and I suppose that we ought to give bonus time for parents who have twins or triplets," offered Pat.

"And we might need to give more time off to a single parent," suggested Harriet.

"Yes, that would only seem fair. We probably ought to take into consideration what the spouse does, too."

"Why would we do that?"

"Well, if the spouse worked at home, that might lessen the need for our associate to have time off. And we may need to treat adoptions differently, too. If parents adopt an older child, he or she may be in school during the day and may require less parenting."

"This is starting to get pretty complicated," observed Lance.

"Yes, I suppose we'll need an IPC," said David.

"IPC?"

"Internal Parenting Code."

"Y'know, I think the problem that complicates everything is that the partners are not on-board with the idea of parenting leave. This whole thing would be a lot easier if they were," said Harriet. "We might not even need an IPC."

"Yes, trouble is that our partners have all been through this and didn't have the advantage of this kind of leave. Most of them now are either past the time when they can have children, or have more sense than to do it again, so they don't see anything in it for them."

"Hey, I've got an idea that might be attractive to partners and make this whole thing fly," said Pat.

"What's that?" asked Harriet.

"Grandparenting leave."

Under Your Wing

To stem the rising tide of associate defections, the Committee on Associate Retention and Evaluation (CARE), deliberated on possible revisions to the Firm's non-operative mentorship program. During the approximately eight months during which these deliberations took place, another sixteen associates departed the Firm for greener pastures. Eventually, CARE memorialized their conclusions, which are set forth below.

TO: ALL LAWYERS
FROM: CARE
RE: MENTORSHIP PROGRAM
It has not escaped our attention that during the past three years the Firm has experienced a greater than optimum associate attrition situation, which has resulted in the redeployment of some fifty odd (and eight normal) former associates to other venues. We are concerned with this situation for several reasons, which are presented below, in no particular order:

1. attrition results in a personal cost to the attriting associate;
2. attrition results in a personal cost to non-attriting attorneys;
3. attrition results in a whopping big financial cost to the partners of this firm.

Actually, now that we look at the list, they do seem to be in order: reverse order of importance to the Firm.

From interviews, focus groups, questionnaires, and divination, we have concluded that a major contributor to our attrition has been the lack of a fully viable mentorship program. After careful study, we have concluded some things that we want to tell you all about in this memo.

History of Mentorship

Mentorship started way back in ancient Greece, with Harry Mentor, an old guy who developed physical problems that resulted in the first, unrecorded hip replacement operation. After that, he needed a lot of help, and when people would ask what the problem was, they were told it was Mentor's hip. Later, the two words were combined, and, in 243 BCE the " ' " and the space were dropped.

Over time, the phrase "mentorship" was broadened beyond helping people with their hips. Fast-forwarding a bit here, mentorship became a very big deal in law firms. In large law firms around the country, it became common for older guys to take younger guys "under their wing" in order to "teach them the ropes." This worked better when there were all guys, but it continued even after that period.

In the good old days, mentoring just sorta happened. No big fuss was made about it. The reasons that mentorship just sorta happened then and doesn't just sorta happen now can be summarized as follows:

1. In the good old days, firms were smaller;
2. In the good old days, mentors and mentees shared the same gender;
3. In the good old days, there was less pressure to bill;
4. In the good old days, clients were really, really stupid and let large law firms take young lawyers along to meetings and court, and bill their time while they were just sitting there, watching what was going on.

Now all of the things that made mentoring just sorta happen don't exist anymore, which pretty much brings us up to the present day, and accounts for the dilemma that now faces us.

Mentorship Issues

In developing the mentorship program that will be described later, CARE considered a number of issues. Those issues, and a little something we thought about those issues, are listed right after the following colon:

1. Should mentorship just be allowed to happen naturally? After much debate, CARE decided that it should not be allowed to happen naturally. Our reasoning was that it does not happen naturally.

2. Should mentors be assigned within an associate's practice area, or outside of his practice area? Here, after due deliberation, CARE decided that the answer was "yes."

3. Should associates be assigned a partner as a mentor, or should senior associates act as mentors? On the side of having partners as mentors, it was argued that it "just seemed right" that partners, rather than associates, should be mentors. On the side of having senior associates as mentors was the possibility that associates might actually do something to mentor. CARE opted to do what seemed right.

4. Should only partners who volunteer to be mentors act as mentors? Those in favor of this position argued that you really only want people who want to do the job. Those opposed pointed out that a partner would have to be crazy to volunteer to be a mentor, and the Firm did not want crazy mentors. CARE opted for forced mentorship.

5. Should male partners be allowed to mentor women, or should the Firm adopt a womentoring program for women? Those who said that women should mentor women argued that they would be able to relate better to one another. Those on the opposite side pointed out that with the number of women partners we have, each partner would have to womentor fourteen associates. CARE decided to mix the sexes and see what happened.

6. Should minority partners mentor minority associates, or should any partner be allowed to mentor a minority associ-

ate? Discussion on this point was quite heated for several hours, until somebody pointed out that the Firm does not have any minority partners. While this did not dissuade several CARE members from wanting to debate the issue further, CARE ultimately ruled, 6-5, that the issue was moot.

7. Should the Firm use retired or semi-retired partners to mentor associates? Those who thought we should use retired or semi-retired partners as mentors pointed out that these people had a wealth of experience they could share, and that they were not that busy, so had the time to mentor. Those opposed pointed out that many of those in this category had turned senile and thus might not make ideal mentors. They also pointed out that some semi-retired partners would be included, in any case, since a number of the partners had simply not announced that they were semi-retired and continued to take their full draw. CARE decided that retired or semi-retired partners were not partners and thus should not be included as mentors.

8. Should time spent by partners in mentoring associates be treated the same as billable time? Those who thought the time should be treated as billable argued that making the time billable would increase the likelihood that partners would take the responsibility seriously. Those opposed pointed out the adverse effect that such a policy would have on the Firm's bottom line, because partners would have fulfilled their billable time obligations with time that could not actually be billed. The resultant decline in the bottom line would cause the most productive partners to leave the Firm, which would cause there to be fewer partners available to mentor. They also pointed out the absurdity of suggesting that partners would take their mentorship responsibilities seriously. CARE decided that mentoring time would not be treated as billable, but that mentors would receive full credit for time spent mentoring, in another life.

9. How should partner-associate mentor-mentee relations be assigned? Some committee members suggested that individual associates' and partners' interests, personalities, law

schools, colleges and the like be utilized in determining the best matches. Others argued that this would be an enormous task. CARE determined that all partner names should be put in one hat and all associate names in another, and that those names should be pulled out, one by one, and matches made in this way. To assure that the process is fair, the drawing will be held in public, and will be supervised by an accounting firm.

Duties of Mentor

CARE feels that a mentor is most likely to fulfill his or her duties if those duties are clearly understood and specified. Accordingly, CARE has embarked upon a mission to define mentors' duties. Unfortunately, this cannot be accomplished overnight. Fort Wayne, Indiana was not built in a day, after all. We hope to have the list of mentor duties to you by the end of the year, or at least by the following autumn.

> NOTE: Prior to the time that CARE completed its work in defining mentors' duties, the economic climate deteriorated, associates stopped leaving the Firm, and the mentorship program was dropped.

A Game of Chance

"So, that's the story, Manny," concluded Annabelle Under-Appreciated, the Firm's loyal Director of Recruitment, exasperated. "We plan this party to boost morale around the office—to get associates and partners together, at this fun place, Gilligan's, with games and good food and everything—and I can't get people to come." (Though associate morale technically is outside the scope of Annabelle's jurisdiction as Director of Recruitment, the price she pays for her competence is that the scope of her jurisdiction is irrelevant.)

"What seems to be the problem, Annabelle?"

"Oh, everybody's got some excuse. Some say they're too busy, some don't like the time the party's called for—either too early, cutting into the work day, or too late, since it will keep them away from spouses and kids. And some just plain don't want to kill four or five hours with the lawyers from this office."

"Well, we've already announced the party, and billed it as a morale booster. We can't just cancel it, Annabelle, can we?"

"No, I think we've got to come up with some incentive for people to attend."

Emanuel Candoo, Chair of the Committee for Associate Retention and Evaluation (CARE), lapsed into thought, then unlapsed suddenly, shouting, "I've got it, Annabelle. We'll give them some incentive to attend."

"Great idea, Manny."

"Here's what we'll do. We'll hold a raffle, offer two round-trip, first-class plane tickets to any place in the United States. The catch is that you have to be present at the party to win the tickets. I'll have to run this by our managing partner, but I think I can sell it to Steve. Why don't you come along."

Manny and Annabelle walked down to the spacious corner office of managing partner Stephen Falderall. "Steve, you know our Director of Recruitment, Annabelle Under-Appreciated, don't you?"

"'Course I know Annabelle; she's the only one who gets anything done around this place. What's on your mind, Manny?"

"It's about the party we're having at Gilligan's."

"That damn thing. Had to cancel a dinner party and a client meeting so I could boost the morale of a bunch of overpaid associates. What is it?"

"Well, we're having trouble getting people to attend..."

"You are? Well, I'll just crack their heads together and..."

"Ah, Mr. Falderall, that may not exactly help morale."

"You're right, Annabelle."

"So," continued Manny, "what we were thinking was that we'd offer a couple first-class air tickets in a raffle, to encourage attendance."

"Prizes to attend a morale party? You've got to be kidding. Who's going to pay for the tickets?"

"There's enough money available in our entertainment budget, Mr. Falderall."

"Then your entertainment budget is too damn high. ... Oh, okay, just go ahead, I don't have time for this. Only make sure that one of our star associates wins the raffle."

"Oh, we won't be able to do that, Steve. The drawing's got to be on the up and up. And the winner may not even be an associate. We're also having trouble attracting partners to this thing, so I'm intending to make them eligible for the raffle as well."

"Holy Christopher, what are we coming to? On the other hand, maybe Paulette and I will win the raffle. That would make it the first Firm party she ever enjoyed."

Manny and Annabelle left Steve's office, confident that attendance at the party would soar with the announcement of the raffle, and that everything would once again be both peaches and cream at their happy firm.

The day before the party, however, Annabelle and Manny found themselves back in the managing partner's office.

"Bad news, Steve. We've got some morale problems that seem to have been caused by our morale party," Manny announced.

"Now what's the problem?"

"Well, Steve, the associates had several difficulties with the raffle."

"Such as?"

"First of all, they didn't like the idea that partners were included. They think that partners earn so much more than associates that they can afford to pay for flights to wherever they want to go."

"Did you explain to them the rationale for including partners?"

"Yes."

"And what did they say?"

"They understood the rationale, but they still didn't think it was fair."

"Not fair, I see. ... And what other problems did the little darlings have?"

"They were concerned that the raffle be conducted honestly."

"Why, the little ingrates. Don't they trust us?"

"Well, Mr. Falderall, you did suggest that we make sure one of the star associates won it," Annabelle reminded him.

"I was just kidding, damnit."

"Well, we've solved that problem, anyway. Our accountants have agreed to act as raffle monitors, for a modest fee. And associates on the Morale Committee have declared themselves ineligible to win the prize."

"Why the hell did they do that?"

"Because they've seen all those giveaways in which employees of the company offering the prize are ineligible," Annabelle explained.

"The associates are also upset that only those present can win," added Manny, "since some associates will be unable to attend because they're out of town on client business."

"But if we give the prize to somebody who doesn't attend, we'll defeat the whole reason for the raffle," Steve reminded them. "And besides, some people probably could make it back into town in time for the party, but wouldn't if they'd be eligible for the raffle, anyway."

"We could give four coach tickets and have one set for those attending and one for those out of town on client business," suggested Manny.

"And make *everyone* unhappy," said Steve.

"How about this: to check on associates who say they're out of town because they can't attend, we could have partners certify that the associate had to be away and couldn't make it back for the party," suggested Manny.

"Sure. What incentive would the partner have not to certify that the associate had to be away? Unless, of course, you want to suggest that we establish penalties for false certification, and a procedure for determining the accuracy of certifications? And what about *partners* who are out of town on business? Who would certify *their* unavailability—clients?"

"Oh, the associates don't think that out-of-town partners should be eligible," said Annabelle.

"Let me guess, Annabelle. They think it's 'not fair.'"

"Yes, Mr. Falderall. And I'm starting to get some rumblings about this raffle from partners, too."

"No, spare me," said Steve.

"Some partners are concerned about whether the raffle violates state gaming statutes. They've asked an associate to research the matter. Two tax partners are trying to structure the raffle in a way that would make the tickets non-taxable to the winner. And a few of the partners who are attending got wind of the associates' suggestion that those out of town on business be included, and they're objecting on the ground that it would decrease their chances of winning. And several gay associates tell me they're thinking of organizing a boycott of the party because the owner of the restaurant we're having it at is suspected of being a homophobe."

Just then Firm patriarch Stanley J. Fairweather walked into Steve's office. Steve explained to Stanley what had happened and asked, "Help us out here. What do you think: should associates and partners be eligible, or just associates; and only those who attend or those who are out of town on client business, too?"

"First of all, the idea of holding a party to boost Firm morale strikes me as bizarre. Everyone knows that the worst thing you can do for morale around this place is to have people at the Firm socialize. But I guess we're beyond that, so I'd go with your original plan, Steve. Everyone who actually attends is eligible — period."

"But what about all the associates who say it's unfair?" asked Manny. "And if everyone's so unhappy with this, won't we defeat the goal of improving morale?"

"Tell our associates that life is unfair, and if this is as unfair as it gets for them, they're plenty lucky. And if this ruins the morale at the Firm, then maybe our Morale Committee wasn't such a good idea. We should stick to practicing law."

Dressing for Success

"It's gone too far this time, Annabelle."

"What's gone too far?"

"I happened to be down here late last night, after eleven, because I have this big deal that I'm trying to close. And I saw six or eight associates walking down the hall."

"And you're upset that so many of them were here so late? How humane of you, Sherwood. Did you tell them to go home and get to bed?"

"I was *not* upset to see them. That's what they're supposed to be doing, with the salaries we're paying them. And I didn't have to tell them to prepare for bed, they already had."

"What on earth are you talking about, Sherwood?"

"They were walking down the hall, and they, they, they had.... pajamas on."

"You're kidding, aren't you?"

"I wish I were."

"So they were just barefoot, in their pajamas, walking down the hall?"

"No, they weren't barefoot, they had slippers on. Rebecca had some of those high-heel jobs, with the feathers all over them."

"Aren't you being a bit sexist there, Sherwood, commenting on Rebecca's slippers?"

"I am not being sexist. The damn feathers are besides the point. The point is that they were walking down the hall in pajamas and bedroom slippers. Two of them had bathrobes on."

"So did you confront them about this?"

"I was too dumbfounded at first to say anything. When I regained my composure, though, I tracked them down in the cafeteria."

"What were they doing there?"

"Having milk and cookies."

"That sounds appropriate. Did you talk to them about the pajamas issue?"

"I most certainly did."

"And what did they say?"

"They said it was part of the new casual dress policy."

"But the casual dress policy doesn't say anything about permitting pajamas, does it?"

"My argument exactly, but they didn't buy it."

"What did they say?"

"They said that while the letter of the casual dress policy didn't specifically permit pajamas, the spirit of the new policy is to make attorneys comfortable, and that after ten there's nothing more comfortable than pajamas. Therefore, in keeping with the intent of the framers of the casual dress policy, they were dressing in pajamas."

"But weren't you the principal framer of the policy?"

"I pointed that out to them. Perhaps I needn't have called myself the Thomas Jefferson of the casual dress policy, but I wanted to drive the point home."

"And what did they say to that?"

"That the intent of the framers is more complicated than I thought. It has to be ascertained in the light of the current situation, and the actual framers' opinions were likely to be biased."

"Well, they certainly went to law school, didn't they."

"I'm sorry we caved in on this whole casual dress thing, anyway."

"But remember, we had to do it. The decision was driven by the impact on recruitment. Students wanted to be able to dress casually."

"I don't think that was what drove it."

"Okay then, it was clients who drove it. They're all dressing casually now."

"So what. You don't have to dress the same way your clients do. Judges and clergy still wear robes. Policemen wear uniforms. Getting dressed up was our uniform. It gave us a certain dignity and decorum."

"So who did drive it, then?"

"My personal theory is that it was the clothing industry. They needed a way to make people buy whole new wardrobes, so they invented this whole 'business casual' oxymoron. 'Business casual' makes about as much sense as 'beach formal.'"

"Whoever invented it, what harm does it do, Sherwood?"

"For one thing, it puts us in the position of legislating clothing—khakis are okay, or not, shoes must not be open-toed or tennis. Who needs it!"

"But that'll sort itself out pretty quickly, and nobody'll think about it anymore."

"Another thing is that you can't tell who are lawyers and who works in the mailroom. In fact, when somebody is well dressed these days, I assume they work in the mailroom."

"Why do you need to know who works in the mailroom and who is a lawyer? Is the problem that you now have to treat everybody like a human being?"

"Ooh, that was a low blow, Annabelle. There are reasons for wanting to know who the lawyers are at a law firm. In fact, I think the casual dress policy has led to a decline in civility around the Firm."

"How so?"

"I think that when you dress casually, you act casually. You've got a street-clothes mentality and you're just not as polite and civil as you are when you're dressed up."

"Sherwood, I never thought of you as an old fuddy-duddy, but you are, aren't you?"

"See what I mean, Annabelle? You never used to call me an old fuddy-duddy before business casual."

"No, but you didn't used to be one."

"Your name calling isn't going to make me back down, nor am I not going to lower myself to calling you names."

"Is that because you're wearing a coat and tie?"

"Maybe, in part. I also think that dressing casually encourages a less professional approach to your legal work and to your clients. You behave the way you do in part because of the way you dress."

"Well, even if you're right, Sherwood, isn't all of this just crying over spilled milk? We're not going to go backwards, are we?"

"First of all, I wouldn't call it going backwards. But in any case, I wouldn't be so sure that we're locked into this. It might actually be a great recruiting idea to go back to 'business usual.'"

"How so?"

"Well, law students are always looking for something that distinguishes one firm from the next. Law firms being such lemmings, we've all fallen into line: everybody is now business casual. If our firm went back to business usual, it would differentiate us."

"In a negative way."

"Not necessarily. It's all in the marketing, Annabelle. We could sell ourselves as a more professional, civil, respectful place. That ought to attract some students. Then to show our concern for young associates' comfort, after a year or two we could permit casual Fridays during the summer, then Fridays year round and, eventually, go to casual summers."

"But that's where we've been."

"Exactly. By going to business usual fulltime, we can get back to the reasonable business casual we were already at, and make that seem like a big concession to associate concerns."

"That's not going to solve your pajama problem, though, Sherwood."

"No, but I think I've got an idea."

"I'm ready. Shoot."

"We come up with a classy royal blue robe with the Firm logo on it, and matching bedroom slippers. But I'm not moving off of the 'no curlers' rule, Annabelle, even if you do think that's sexist."

Gym Dandy

CHIP, the Fairweather, Winters & Sommers Committee on Health in Practice, was listening to – and interrupting regularly – the head of the Firm's workout facility, Rocky, who was giving one of his periodic reports to the committee. A transcript of the discussion appears below:

"So, I think we got a pretty good gym set-up now, what with the free weights, the expensive weights, the stairmasters, the rowing machines, the stationary bikes, the spinning machines, the treadmills and all; we're doin' pretty good."

"You mean we bought all of that equipment, Rocky?"

"Yup."

"Wasn't that terribly expensive?"

"Yup. We're thinking about expanding, though. Some of the ladies and the gentlemen, they want separate facilities."

"Why's that?"

"I guess they don't want to show each other how flabby they are."

"But didn't we approve sweatsuits with the Firm logo on them? Doesn't that cover up the flab?"

"Not entirely. You ever take a good look at some of your partners? Anyway, lots of them don't wear the sweats, they like the tight spandex stuff."

"Do the associates seem to be taking advantage of and enjoying the gym, Rocky? As I recall, we built this whole thing largely at their behest."

"Well, I wouldn't say they was entirely happy, to tell ya the honest to goodness truth."

"What's their problem?"

"Well, a couple things. They think that we need more staff in the gym, to help them out with their workouts."

"You mean they want personal trainers?"

"Yeah, that's right, except they're callin' 'em 'physical fitness mentors,' I think."

"What else are they unhappy with, Rocky?"

"The hours. I get a lot of complaints about the hours. They think the place oughta be open 24/7, 'cause that's what they work."

"Is that it?"

"Pretty much, except that, of course, they want a whirlpool, sauna, and steam room in both the ladies' and the gents' locker rooms. And there's been some talk I heard lately about how we maybe ought to put in a swimming pool."

"A swimming pool? That's the most ridiculous idea I ever heard of. These associates just don't get it, do they? I mean, don't they know we're running a law firm here, not a health spa."

"Actually, I think it was Mr. Fairweather who mentioned the swimming pool idea. He swims half a mile every morning."

"Oh. Uh, in that case, Rocky, I think a swimming pool's an excellent idea. I mean, why scrimp? If you're going to do it, do it right, I always say."

"And speaking of a health spa, I almost forgot, there's been some complaints about there not bein' no masseuses or nothin', and no herbal wraps and mud baths. I think somebody said somethin' about smell treatments, too."

"Smell treatments?"

"I think Rocky must mean aromatherapy."

"Yeah, that's it, aromas. And another thing is that they want fresh fruit and juices around for after their workouts."

"Don't you get frustrated with all of these complaints, Rocky?"

"Me? No, I don't frustrate, I work out. Besides, I think we're makin' some really good progress at the gym, which gives me a great deal of personal satisfaction."

"Progress? What kind of progress are you talking about?"

"Well, we've got the average weight of bench pressin' up about 20 pounds in the last month or so, and our curls are up in weight and repetitions, the body fat is comin' down pretty much on target, and…"

"Wait a minute. You've got goals for people, targets?"

"No, they ain't targets, exactly. Everybody's gotta hit 'em. If they don't, we keep 'em in the gym extra time, until they do."

"How did we start doing that, Rocky?"

"Well, it's in keepin' with the whole idea of the gym in the first place. The Firm decided that it was in their interest to have healthy lawyers. They figured the healthier they are, the more stamina they'll have and the more hours they can work and the longer they can live, and that all of that's in the Firm's interest in makin' the big bucks, if you catch my drift."

"So you've set up these goals, and every associate has got to meet them?"

"Yup."

"Well, at least they have some definable targets and good and accurate feedback. They don't get much of that in the rest of their practice."

"For sure, they get feedback. I can guarantee that, 'cause I been sittin' in on their reviews."

"You mean, when we evaluate them, you're in on it?"

"Yup. You might say they get mental feedback and physical feedback. I'm the physical part."

"Thanks for clarifying that, Rocky."

"Happy to do it, that's what I'm here for."

"And what exactly do you tell them?"

"I tell them where they need to improve, and we set goals for the next review. Some of them is doin' a lot better on the physical part than the mental part, if you know what I mean, so some of your partners are hintin' to them that their best future might be in that particular physical line of work and not the more mental stuff."

"Well, I admire the honest feedback that we're giving them, but I'm afraid that we've gotten away from the main purpose of why we set up this gym."

"Meanin' what?"

"Meaning that I thought we set up the gym because people needed a release. They needed some relaxation."

"Yup."

"And instead of that, we seem to be giving them more strain and competitiveness in their lives, more goals to reach, more opportunities for failure."

"I think Sara has a point, Rocky. Maybe we're overdoing this gym thing. Do you have any suggestions, Sara?"

"I do. I think we need to rethink our whole approach. I'd pull out all of that fancy exercise equipment and put in sandboxes, in which our attorneys could learn how to share toys and to play well with others. Then I'd add some swings, on which they could go 'wheeeee' and feel a sense of freedom."

"Good idea, Sara. And we could install some carousels, because a lot of what we do as lawyers is go round and round anyway. To make the carousels seem more realistic to our lawyers, we could use limousines rather than painted ponies."

"We could bring in some 3-wheeler bikes rather than those spinning machines, so that our lawyers would have a sense that they were getting someplace."

"And we could hire somebody kind, to comfort them when they got owies."

"Owies?"

"Yes, owies, Rocky, when they hurt themselves. And we could tell them it's okay for them to cry every once in awhile, to show their emotions. Then we'd have something really different from other firms, and we'd be giving our lawyers what they need—a little human attention and kindness."

"Whoa, I'm gettin' outa here. You guys are goin' nuts."

"Bye, Rocky. Bye-bye."

The Black Hole of Belugessi

Having finally closed his mega real estate deal, Fairweather, Winters & Sommers associate Tom Wisham returned to writing the story of Hotchkiss & Raxo, P.C. lawyers Brick Rhodes, Lucy Prod, Lou Dembitz, and Pamela Goya, who had been sent to rescue their brethren on the planet Iota IV.

Wham! Grrankz! Flopsch!

Spaceship Gavel plunged into the Black Hole of Belugessi, hitting the curved wall and winding its way gradually clockwise down and around the cylindrical inner wall, settling eventually on the bottom. "Is everyone okay?" asked Dembitz.

"A little dizzy, but otherwise alright," said Brick.

"Peachy," answered Lucy, "just peachy."

"What about you, Pamela?" asked Dembitz. And then, "Pamela!"

Pamela came to and shook her head. "Where am I, what the hell is going on here?"

"Relax, Pamela," said Dembitz, "you're okay, that is, as okay as anyone could be in the Black Hole of Belugessi. You were just temporarily stunned by the impact of hitting the Hole. We'd better start exploring this place. Brick, why don't you take a walk outside."

"Wait a minute, why me?"

"Process of elimination, Brick. Lucy and me are partners. It'd be insanity to send a partner out on anything that danger- ous. Partners work behind the scenes, take the credit when things go right. Associates do the tough work, take the risks. Outer space doesn't change that. And Pamela here is still recuperating. So you're it."

Brick made his way slowly to the rear of the ship, said his goodbyes to his comrades, and slid out the hatch. He felt disoriented. He could see nothing.

"That your buggy, Bub?"

Brick was startled by the voice. He looked around, but saw no one.

"I said, 'That your buggy, Bub?' Are you thick of ear, Bub? Eustachian tube tied? anvil out to lunch? stirrup need adjustin'? doggie got your incus? I'm talkin' to you, Bub."

"Sorry, I didn't see you."

"'Course you didn't, you're new in the Hole, aren't you?"

"Yes, just got in."

"Haven't had your peeper-plant then, have ya?"

"What?"

"Peeper-plant, so you can get yourself a pair a' winkers that work."

"No, I haven't had a chance yet. Where do you get one?"

"Peeperologist, of course. Make sure you get yourself a peeperologist, though, not an orbologist. Some people get confused. Now, you haven't answered my question: is that your buggy?"

"Well, I guess you could say so. I don't own it, but me and three others flew it in here. Why?"

"Gotta slap a ticket on ya.'"

"A ticket? What kind of a ticket?"

"Contra-Rubric clockwise swirl."

"What?"

"You still having trouble with those ears, Bub? I said, 'Contra-Rubric clockwise swirl.' When you came into the Hole, you hit the wall and swirled down clockwise. That's against the Rubric. So I'm going to have to issue you a little citation."

"But I had no idea that that was against the, er, Rubric."

"You didn't see the circular sign with a clockwise swirl and a line drawn through it diagonally, the intergalactic no-clockwise-swirling sign?"

"No I didn't see it. It was pitch black, I couldn't see a thing."

"That's not my fault. Bub."

"Well, it's not my fault, either."

"Look, Bub, I don't make the Rubric. The Rubric's the Rubric, that's all there is to it. You're not the first one to have this happen to you. In fact, everyone who falls into the Hole gets slapped with a citation. Gravity makes you go 'round clockwise. So you're not being discriminated against. The Rubric's fair."

"If everybody violates the Rubric and nobody can help it, then why isn't the Rubric changed? Nobody's hurt by people swirling clockwise."

"Just because others do it, don't make it right. Didn't your mommy ever teach you that? And besides, harm's got nothin' to do with it, it's a matter of revenue. We need the fines. Like I say, Bub, I don't make the Rubric, I just enforce it."

"But I wasn't even flying the ship, Dembitz was. How can you give me a ticket? That's guilt by association."

"What's wrong with that? If everyone made sure that the people they associate with obeyed the Rubric, we'd all be a lot better off. Guilt by association just encourages everyone to keep an eye on his pals."

"This is outrageous. I demand a trial. I know my rights."

"Okay, go ahead."

"What do you mean, 'okay, go ahead'?"

"I mean, go ahead with the trial. I'm a rubricist. I hear the cases."

"You what? *You* hear the cases? But you just gave me the ticket, how can you give me a fair trial? Why don't we have an impartial judge, bailiffs, court reporters, lawyers, jurors, the whole schmear?"

"Watch your step, Bub, you're comin' dangerously close to impugning the integrity of a rubricist, namely me, and I don't think you want to get hit with that charge. The B-H-double B-A wouldn't take kindly to that, I'm afraid."

"Who's the B-H-double B-A?"

"The Black Hole of Belugessi Bar Association. They rated me 'well qualified' in their last evaluation of rubricists. And as to why we don't have the cast of characters that you rattled off, why the hell should we? Why should Belugessians bear the cost of all of that for a simple little trial in which everybody knows that the defendant is guilty as hell? Now, are you ready to get on with this?"

"I suppose. I didn't and couldn't see your sign; even if I could, there was nothing that I could have done to go counter-clockwise; no harm was done to anyone, and so I respectfully say that there is no reason why I should be found guilty."

"I have considered your arguments and I am persuaded that you are right, there *is* no reason why you should be found guilty."

"Good, now is there any way to get out of here?"

"Wait a minute, not so fast, Bub. Since no reason is required for you to be found guilty (as we say here in the Hole, 'Justice is deaf') and since you have clearly violated the Rubric, I find you guilty. Now for the sentencing ..."

"Wait a minute, I want to appeal."

"Terribly sorry, Bub, no appeal. A matter of economics. Appeals from a minor matter like this just aren't worth the time. You may, though, want to consider getting some help for the sentencing."

"You mean a lawyer?"

"We call them rubrictwisters."

"Why would I need one? What kind of sentence could I get?"

"The max would be a fine of six blues, three reds, and two yellows (which comes to about $42,000, U.S.) and fourteen years in a room with no bed and only bread and Orange Frizz."

"Why in the world would somebody be put away for fourteen years for a contra-Rubric clockwise swirl?"

"Rehabilitation."

"Rehabilitation? Why the hell do I need rehabilitation for following the laws of gravity? And what kind of rehabilitation is that, anyway, fourteen years on bread and Orange Frizz?"

"By now, you know the answer to why you need rehabilitation – I don't make the Rubric. As to the particular rehabilitation, we have found that all rehabilitation is imperfect. Recidivism is high. By putting you in the jug for fourteen years, we know that you're not going to make a contra-Rubric clockwise for that long, which makes our crime statistics and penal policy look pretty good. As to the no bed, the bread and the Orange Frizz, those are purely economic; beds don't grow on trees, bread is cheap, and the Liege Lord of the Black Hole has a hefty investment in the Orange Frizz Beverage Company in Biloxi, Mississippi, Earth."

"Okay, maybe I'd better get myself a rubrictwister. Where do I get one?"

"I'm a rubrictwister, Bub. I'll need a retainer, though."

"A retainer? How much?"

"Six blues, three reds, and two yellows."

"But that's the maximum amount you said I could be fined."

"Good rubrictwisters don't come cheap. If you want some schlock rubrictwister, go ahead. You get what you pay for."

"Never mind, I'll take you. Do you accept checks?"

"With two major credit cards and a driver's license."

Brick took out his identification and wrote the check in the dark. "Now, can we do the sentencing?"

"Sure. What have you got to say for yourself, Bub?"

"What have *I* got to say? I thought that the rubrictwister I just paid $42,000 to would say something on my behalf."

"Charmed, Bub. Your rubricist, may it please the court, the defendant is a first-time offender, he wasn't doing the flying, and he was helpless in the face of gravity. I ask that you be merciful."

"Well said, counsel. The defendant will be fined three reds, six blues, and two yellows. There will be no prison sentence, and the matter will not appear on the defendant's record."

"Well, at least I avoided the jail sentence."

"That's a laugh. You didn't really think that I was going to give you a jail sentence, do you?"

"But all of that stuff about rehabilitation..."

"You fell for that? Pure baloney. You have to talk about rehabilitation to make the system seem respectable. Cash, that's what we're after. And a little retribution, too. Rehabilitation is for the Rubric Reviews."

"So you mean that I didn't do any better hiring you as a rubrictwister than I would have done on my own?"

"You pays your money, you takes your chances, Bub. I never promised you results. You wouldn't want me to use undue influence on the rubricist, would you?"

"What was that stuff the rubricist said about the conviction not appearing on my record?"

"That means two things; first, you're not officially a criminal, haven't crossed the Rubric-con, so to speak, and second, it won't affect your insurance rates. You do have insurance, don't you?"

"No, I don't, but I suppose that you could fix me up with some. Are you an insurance agent, too?"

"Absolutely not, that would be a conflict of interest."

Just then an earshattering, "Clanktsh, Grrrooomst, Grrooomst" sounded above, and Brick stopped himself in midquestion. "What was that horrible noise?"

"Your ship, Bub. They're towing it away, it was parked contra-Rubrically."

"Where will they take it?"

"Most likely to the Croncher. Space is tight around here. Contra-Rubric parking's a serious offense. They crush the offending vehicle."

"But it's not just the vehicle, it's Lou Dembitz and Lucy Prod and Pamela Goya, they're in there."

"Sorry, Bub, I don't make the Rubric. Gotta run, just saw another poor sucker make a contra-Rubric clockwise, looks like another six blues, three reds, and two yellows for the Belugessi coffers. So long."

"Wait a minute! Where is the Peeperologist? I can't see a thing and I've got to get to the Croncher before it crushes my poor friends!"

Note: Wisham's secretary sent this chapter to her uncle in Hollywood, where Wisham is now happily employed. He has hired the Fairweather firm to represent him, and he relishes ordering his former bosses around. Seventeen other Fairweather associates are now secretly working on space serials.

Freedom to Associate

"The associates want a committee," said Emanuel Candoo, Chair of CARE, the Committee on Associate Retention and Evaluation.

"But they have a committee; *we're* their committee," replied Harriet Akers.

"They say they want their own committee, though," said the Chair.

"Well, I've got an idea," said Lance Byte.

"What?"

"Why don't we tell them that they can't have their own committee?" suggested Lance Byte.

"We can't do that," said Harriet. "That would be saying no to our associates."

"And what's wrong with that?" asked David Alms. "We say no to our children."

"Associates aren't children," said Patrick Conshenz. "They're young adults. Rich young adults, with what we pay them."

"Why do they say they need a committee of their own?" asked Otto Flack.

"They say that they need to have a voice."

"A voice?" said Lance. "I hadn't noticed that they're exactly silent, or hoarse. We seem to hear from them several times every week about whatever is on their precious little minds."

"No, but they say that they don't have an *official* voice, and they point out that a lot of other firms have established associates committees," said the Chair.

"Exactly who do they expect to be on this committee?" asked David.

"I think we've got some flexibility there," said the Chair. "They haven't specified."

"Nice of them to give us some flexibility," commented David.

"Okay, so, no problem. We just appoint a bunch of associates who are wimps, the kind that are beholden to us, and we beknight them as the associates committee," said Lance.

"I doubt that that will fly," said Patrick. "I suspect that they're going to want to elect their own committee members."

"Elect them? What the hell do they think this is, a democracy? We partners don't even elect our Executive Committee, they just reappoint themselves."

"Yes, this is going to turn into a union, if we're not careful," cautioned David. "Maybe we should have a few partners on the committee."

"No, they're not going to want anyone from management," said Patrick.

"Isn't it important that we have some associate representation from all the different constituencies?" asked Harriet.

"That's a good point. We'll want at least one from each of the departments," said the Chair.

"And we'll want diversity in terms of sex, sexual orientation, race, nationality, religion, and creed," pointed out Harriet.

"What's creed?"

"Never mind, Patrick."

"And we certainly are going to want associates from each of the different classes," said Lance.

"And we can't forget the different offices," reminded the Chair.

"How are we going to assure all of that diversity?" asked David.

"I suppose that we could have separate elections, by class, by department, by office, by sex and the like. That would assure diversity," offered Patrick.

"Yes, and it would also assure the most complicated election apparatus in world history," replied David.

"I'm not opposed to elections, as long as it's by secret ballot and the results are tabulated by our committee," announced Lance.

"You're not suggesting that we would alter the results of a duly and fairly conducted election, are you?" asked Patrick.

"Perish the thought, Pat. Let's just say I've got a good feeling about who might emerge victorious if we count."

"Wait a minute here," said Otto. "I just did some math. We've got six departments, seven associate classes, six different offices and, if you throw in another few for race and religion and creed, whatever that is, and a partridge in a pear tree, we're talking about a committee of over twenty-five associates. Getting them together is going to be pretty expensive."

"How often do you think they'd need to get together?" asked Harriet.

"Maybe once a month," offered Patrick.

"But surely you jest," said David. "I can't imagine them meeting more than once a quarter, at the most."

"How about never? We form the committee, but tell them they can't meet," suggested Lance. "That way we'd give them what they want, an associates committee, but avoid the potential mischief they'd cause by actually meeting."

"I doubt that that one would fly," opined the Chair. "I think that we probably need to allow them to meet at least once a quarter."

"Why don't we require that the meetings be on weekends?" suggested Otto. "That will cut down on the amount of billable time we lose."

"Good idea," said Lance. "That will also test the seriousness of the little bastards in claiming that they need a voice."

"Yes, and we can justify the weekend meeting requirement based on the reduced Saturday night stay-over airfares," added Otto.

"What's the jurisdiction of the committee going to be?" asked David.

"Well, I'd thought they would discuss whatever was of concern to them," said the Chair.

"Are you kidding? Give them carte blanche?" asked Otto. "Not bloody likely."

"I think Otto's right, Manny. We've got to place some limit on what the associates committee discusses," said Harriet. "Any ideas?"

"How about whatever issues are of concern to associates?" suggested Patrick.

"Oh, yes, that will really restrict them," said David. "It will eliminate everything they don't care about."

"What if we give the associates topics on which we want their opinions, and have them deal just with those?" suggested Lance.

"Yes, and we could bug the meeting room to make sure they weren't talking about something we didn't want them to," offered David.

"I don't think we ought to bug the room; it might be unconstitutional or something," said Patrick.

"Astute legal analysis, Pat," said David. "I was just kidding."

"Well, you shouldn't kid about that, it's dangerous."

"Dangerous?"

"Yes, the associates could be bugging this room, and they wouldn't know that what you were suggesting was a joke."

"Even if we can agree on what should be their jurisdiction, we need to decide what their authority is," the Chair reminded the committee.

"Isn't that the same thing?" asked Pat.

"Not exactly, Pat. We can allow them to talk about whatever the hell they want, as long as they can't do anything about it," explained David.

"Well, of course they're not going to have any authority to do anything. Nobody has any authority to do anything in this firm," said Lance.

"Except the Executive Committee," the Chair insisted.

"Of course, except the Executive Committee," said Lance.

"Hey, isn't the creation of an associates committee really a question for the Executive Committee to consider?" asked David.

"But the EC is very busy. If we referred this to them, that could delay the establishment of an associates committee indefinitely," said Patrick.

"Patrick, you're a quick study, you are, my lad," replied David.

Truth and Consequences

Former Fairweather, Winters & Sommers associate Constance Ostrov and Fairweather partner David Alms confronted one another recently on the famous daytime television talk show called *Arnoldo*, which is hosted by Arnoldo Inciterio. We have obtained a transcript of the show, which is set forth in full below.

ARNOLDO: Good afternoon, and welcome to *Arnoldo*, starring me, Arnoldo Inciterio. Today we have what promises to be a fascinating show, giving us a rare inside look into the tawdry world of large law firm life. Please join me now in giving a warm Arnoldo Show welcome to our guests, Constance Ostrov and David Alms.

AUDIENCE MEMBERS: [*Applause and catcalls.*]

ARNOLDO: Thank you both for being with us today. Constance, let's start with you. Tell us something about yourself, will you.

CONSTANCE: Happy to, Arnoldo. I graduated from Yale University, summa cum laude in English Literature, and then went on to Harvard Law School, where I graduated magna cum laude and was editor-in-chief of the Civil Liberties Law Review. After law school, I clerked on the Circuit Court of Appeals for the Second Circuit and then on the United States Supreme Court.

ARNOLDO: Well, you certainly appear to have an outstanding record, Constance, and one to which I'm sure our studio audience can relate, as we typically have a lot of magna graduates of distinguished law schools and former Supreme Court clerks with us in our studio.

AUDIENCE MEMBERS: [*Laughter.*]

ARNOLDO: Tell us how you and Mr. Alms first met, Constance.

CONSTANCE: Mr. Alms interviewed me when I was in my second year at Harvard Law School and was influential in my decision to accept an offer at the Fairweather firm during my second summer.

ARNOLDO: And what did he do to influence your decision?

CONSTANCE: In retrospect, I'd have to say that he sucked up to me shamelessly, telling me that I walked on water, set the sun and raised the moon.

DAVID: I never said those things.

CONSTANCE: Not in so many words, perhaps, but he clearly implied that life was unlikely to be worth living for him and other partners at the firm unless I accepted their offer.

DAVID: We convey that impression to all of our recruits.

ARNOLDO: And why do you do that?

DAVID: Because all of our competitors are doing it, so if we didn't, we wouldn't succeed in attracting the little darlings to our firm.

AUDIENCE MEMBER: So you lied to her.

DAVID: No, I didn't lie. I perhaps overstated a bit, but I certainly never lied.

AUDIENCE MEMBERS: Liar, liar, liar!

DAVID: Even if I did lie, she spent the summer with our firm before she went off to her clerkships, so she knew what she was getting into.

ARNOLDO: What do you have to say about that, Constance? You did spend a summer with the firm before you accepted a permanent offer, didn't you?

CONSTANCE: Yes, Arnoldo, but that only further misled me. They wined me and dined me, took me out to plays and ballgames, and paid me $10,000 a month, so I

thought that was what life would be like when I got
back to the firm.

AUDIENCE MEMBER: Wait a minute. You're a graduate of
Yale and Harvard and you thought that what you got
during the summer was real life? I'm glad I didn't go
to those places, or I might have wound up as stupid as
you.

AUDIENCE MEMBERS: [*Laughter and applause.*]

CONSTANCE: But they misled me, and I feel, well, so violated.

AUDIENCE MEMBER: Honey, have you ever been out on a
date before? Did you swallow every line that your date
fed you? If so, wake up and smell the coffee, 'cause it's
been perkin' a long, long time.

DAVID: That's my point, exactly.

AUDIENCE MEMBER: You shut your trap, Buster. You're no
angel on this, either.

ARNOLDO: Okay, let's get on with this. Constance, tell us
what you found when you returned to the Fairweather
firm after your clerkships.

CONSTANCE: Well, when I came back to the firm, I wound
up working quite a lot with Mr. Alms. And from the
get-go, it was a disaster.

ARNOLDO: Can you tell us what you mean, Constance?
Give us an example or two?

CONSTANCE: Yes, he would call me to come up to his office
and then he'd be on the phone for twenty minutes with
a client.

DAVID: Well, I'm terribly sorry, Constance, but we do have
clients and we do have to take their calls. After all,
they pay the bills, don't they? You could have brought
something with you to my office to work on in case I
got tied up. Or you might have listened to the
conversation I was having, and perhaps even learned
a little something.

CONSTANCE: See what I mean, Arnoldo? Listen to that sarcasm and condescension in his voice. I had to listen to that day in and day out. It got so that I couldn't stand it anymore; I wanted to rip his tongue out.

AUDIENCE MEMBER: Right on, Baby.

DAVID: Is that what they teach you at Harvard as an alternative dispute resolution method, to rip somebody's tongue out?

CONSTANCE: Why, you dirty...

ARNOLDO: C'mon now. Is there anything else, Constance?

CONSTANCE: Yes, plenty. He would give me an assignment, and not tell me all of the facts that I would need to know.

AUDIENCE MEMBER: Ooh, Honey, that *is* bad. Woo, I don't know how in the world you put up with that kind of abuse.

CONSTANCE: She's being sarcastic, too, Arnoldo. Make her stop, make her stop. [*Sobs*]

ARNOLDO: Now, Constance, settle down a bit. You're going to be okay.

DAVID: See, this is the type of mental toughness I got.

AUDIENCE MEMBERS: Hisssss.

CONSTANCE: You haven't heard the half of it. I'd get this rush assignment from him, which would force me to cancel plans that I'd had for months in order to work over the weekend. Then I'd hand in the assignment and it would sit on his desk for two weeks or more, untouched.

ARNOLDO: What do you have to say for yourself, David?

DAVID: Well, Arnoldo, it's possible that something like that may have happened once or twice, but that sort of thing is unavoidable. Emergencies come and go. That's life in the fast lane. And it's not as if she wasn't paid well for it.

CONSTANCE: Paid for it? How much pay is enough for almost ruining your marriage, causing your children to

think that your nanny is their mom? How much is
enough for that, huh?

AUDIENCE MEMBERS: Right on. You tell 'em, Honey. Kick
him in the gnoogies.

CONSTANCE: And then, if there was a mistake, or something
that wasn't quite right, or anything that the client
complained about, he would lay it off on me, or on one
of the other associates, whether it was our fault or not.

ARNOLDO: Is that true, David?

DAVID: Of course it's true. Partners don't make mistakes.
Part of what we pay associates so much for is to take
the blame when something goes wrong.

CONSTANCE: Why you dirty.....[*rushes towards Mr. Alms, who
ducks underneath the coffee table behind which he was
sitting*]

AUDIENCE MEMBERS: Get him. Kick him in the gnoogies.

ARNOLDO: [*stepping between Constance and David*] Come out
from under there, Mr. Alms. Now, please, remember
that you are both officers of the court. Can we please
act with a little dignity and decorum?

CONSTANCE: And it's not just that he blamed us for
everything that went wrong, he took all of the credit
for any successes. He never once said to the client,
"Constance really helped me out on this project, I
couldn't have done it without her."

DAVID: Why would I do that? Look where you are now:
you've left us, gone to another firm. This is the
gratitude that I get for all that I've done for you.

CONSTANCE: Well, maybe if you'd given me a little credit
now and then, or even just said, "Thanks, Constance,
you did a good job on that," maybe then I wouldn't
have left the firm.

DAVID: I thought you knew you'd done a good job. If you
hadn't been doing a good job, I would have told you
that.

ARNOLDO: Well, we're almost out of time now. Constance, you said that David's behavior almost ruined your marriage. I'm sure our audience is curious as to whether you've been able to patch things up with your husband since leaving the firm?

CONSTANCE: Oh, yes, David and I are quite happy, aren't we, Snookums?

DAVID: Yes, Peach Pie.

ARNOLDO: Wait a minute, here. You mean you two are married?

CONSTANCE: Sure. David and I fell in love when I was a summer associate at the Fairweather firm, and we got married during my third year in law school.

ARNOLDO: But I don't get it. Why did you stay with him after all that he did to you?

CONSTANCE: That was at work. David's a perfect little sweetheart at home.

The Last Word

At my firm we spend inordinate amounts of time worrying about whether our associates are happy. If you were to ask me why we do this, I'd have to say, "beats the hell out of me."

Nobody guarantees anybody happiness. Hell, even the damn Declaration of Independence claims only the *pursuit* of happiness as an inalienable right.

In fact, I'd worry if our associates were happy. Associates weren't *meant* to be happy. Some of the best times associates have involve going out with other associates to bitch about how unhappy they are. That's how associates bond. That was true forty years ago and it's true today. In other words, associates are happy to be unhappy. If we succeeded in our attempts to make them happy, we'd be depriving them of one of the greatest pleasures of associatehood.

On the positive side, though, there's little likelihood that we'll succeed in making associates happy. Two factors militate in favor of this conclusion: first, most associates don't know what would make them happy, and second, those who do want different things. So if we were to succeed in giving one group of associates what they wanted, we'd make another group unhappy. This comforts me. In fact, it makes me happy.

Stanley J. Fairweather

Partners/The Full Firm

The Retiring Type

Among the many matters that the firm of Fairweather, Winters & Sommers revisited in the light of changing economic conditions was the provision of its partnership agreement that governed retirement of partners. The old provision read: "Retirement shall be mandatory at the age of 70. Notwithstanding the foregoing, retirement shall not be mandatory at the age of 70."

While this old provision had the virtue of being succinct, it had the disadvantage of being somewhat difficult to interpret. Partners who turned 70 and were told that their time had come pointed to the sentence that said that retirement at 70 was not mandatory. And partners who wanted out at 70, but were requested by the Firm to stay on, were hesitant to do so because of the seemingly clear statement in the first sentence of the mandatory retirement provision.

Partners felt that there were other reasons the provision was ripe for revision. For one thing, many believed that the Firm should provide partners an option for early retirement.

Given the widespread interest in considering a revision of the retirement provision, the Executive Committee appointed an ad hoc committee on revision of the retirement provision, which it called The Ad Hoc Committee on Revision of the Retirement Provision of the Fairweather, Winters & Sommers Partnership Agreement. Despite its catchy name, the committee was referred to affectionately around the Firm as The Dead Wood Committee.

Though the history of the debate that swirled around the retirement provision is fascinating (to those who participated in that debate), the compilers of this book found it somewhat less scintillating and elected not to include the full transcript of the debate. Instead, to give readers a sense of the discussion without burdening them with its full weight, we have set forth below the objectives sought to be accomplished and, immediately below each objective, the provision proposed by the committee and an explanation of the provision:

Objective. To provide a succinct, unambiguous provision governing the retirement of partners.

Provision. Retirement from the Firm shall be mandatory on the third Tuesday of the fourth month after the date on which a partner shall have reached his 70th birthday.

Explanation. The third Tuesday of the fourth month was a compromise reached between those who wanted the date to be the actual birthday of the retiring partner and those who wanted the date to be never.

Objective. To provide an option to retire earlier than the age of 70.

Provision. A partner may elect to retire on the third Tuesday of the fourth month after the date on which he or she reaches any birthday after the 57th birthday and before the 70th birthday. This election shall be made by delivering the following statement, signed by the partner: "I retire." The statement shall be dated and shall have attached a certified copy of the partner's birth certificate. Once made, the election to retire shall be irrevocable.

Explanation. The 57th birthday was picked out of a hat that contained the numbers 55 to 65. The requirement of the birth certificate is designed to demonstrate that the

partner is eligible for retirement. The irrevocability
provision was inserted because several lawyers on The
Dead Wood Committee were of the firm opinion that
they didn't want partners diddling with them.

Objective. To make it possible for the Firm to continue to
have the services of partners who have passed their
70th birthday, but who continue to be productive.

Provision. For purposes of the mandatory retirement provisions of this partnership agreement, the Executive
Committee may deem a partner's 70th birthday and any
subsequent birthdays to be his 69th birthday. The
Executive Committee shall indicate such deem annu-
ally by sending the partner a card that says on the
cover "Some People Get Older Every Year" and on the
inside, "But you look the same to us. Happy 69th
Birthday," signed by a majority of the members of the
Executive Committee.

Explanation. The lead-in to the first sentence of this provision is intended to recognize that the Executive
Committee cannot in fact prevent a partner's 70th
birthday from occurring.

Objective. To rid the Firm of unproductive partners before
their 70th birthday.

Provision. Any partner shall be deemed to have elected to
retire before his 70th birthday if the Executive Committee deems such retirement to be advisable. The Executive Committee may make known its decision by email,
by letter, by voice mail, or by cleaning out the partner's
office. In such event: (a) the third Tuesday of the fourth
month after the partner's birthday shall be deemed to
occur whenever the Executive Committee says it has
occurred; (b) the partner shall be deemed to be at least
57 years old; and (c) the partner shall not be entitled to
any retirement benefits.

Explanation. We think this one is pretty darn clear, don't you?

Objective. Not to disadvantage existing partners who might be adversely affected by the changes in the provision.

Provision. Anyone who is a partner at the time of the adoption of this revised provision on retirement and who would be adversely affected by its terms shall be grandparented in under the old provision of the partnership agreement.

Explanation. Given the ambiguous meaning of the old provision, it is hard to see how anyone could determine that he would be adversely affected by the new provision. However, The Dead Wood Committee thought that this provision might help mute opposition to what they were proposing.

Objective. To assure that retiring partners do not become a burden to their spouses and significant others.

Provision. On or before a partner's 60th birthday, he shall apply to the Firm's Hobby Coordinator for certification that he has developed a Qualifying Hobby. A Qualifying Hobby shall mean a hobby or activity that will keep the partner out of the house at least three days a week. In the event that a partner has no Qualifying Hobby, the Hobby Coordinator will work with the partner to develop such a hobby. No partner shall be eligible for early retirement unless the Hobby Coordinator certifies that he has developed a Qualifying Hobby. In the event that a retiring partner has not developed a Qualifying Hobby, the Executive Committee may at its discretion assign the partner a Qualifying Hobby, in which event the retiring partner shall participate enthusiastically in such Qualifying Hobby. A partner may retire without a Qualifying Hobby if he is living alone at the time of his retirement or if all persons in his household certify in writing that they do not mind having him around.

Explanation. This provision was inspired by the fact that under the old retirement provision, the Executive Committee had experienced extreme pressure from the spouses of retiring partners to allow them to continue practicing (or at least to continue coming in to the office) in order to keep them out of the hair of those at home.

Objective. To assure that the retirement of a partner does not disrupt the Firm's representation of the partner's clients.

Provision. After the age of 60, no partner shall talk to, meet with, or socialize with a client of the Firm except in the company of another partner of the Firm of the age of 50 or younger. Any partner found to violate this rule shall be taken to speak to Stanley J. Fairweather. For the purposes of this rule, Stanley J. Fairweather shall be deemed to be eternally 59.

Explanation. Originally, The Dead Wood Committee had suggested a fine for violation of the rule, but the enforcement mechanism adopted was deemed to be infinitely more effective.

Objective. To assure that nobody inadvertently remains a partner after death.

Provision. The date of a partner's death shall be deemed to be his 70th birthday.

Explanation. One can't be too careful.

Much to the surprise of the partners, and to the dismay of the Dead Wood Committee, the revised provision regarding retirement was soundly defeated. Exit polls indicated that in matters of retirement and death, Fairweather, Winters & Sommers partners prefer ambiguity to certainty.

The Party's Over

The Fairweather, Winters & Sommers Committee on Underwriting Party-Like Events (COUPLE) met amid much consternation last Wednesday. COUPLE rules require that the committee meet amid at least some consternation, preferably more than a little. Since the topic to be considered at the meeting was planning the Firm party, plentiful consternation was virtually assured.

The Chair, Emanuel Candoo, began the meeting by noting that somebody had switched around the place cards that designated where committee members should sit. He asked whether anybody would own up to the act. Lance Byte said that he would. The Chair complimented Lance for his honesty. Lance thanked the Chair for his compliment.

The Chair asked Lance why he had altered the seating. Lance said that he had switched the cards of Harriet Akers and Lionel Hartz because he didn't really like sitting next to Harriet. Harriet said that that was plenty okay by her, since she didn't relish sitting next to Lance, anyway.

Lance said that he was hurt by Harriet's comment. The Chair queried Lance as to why he should be hurt by Harriet's comment, since he had admitted that he had not wanted to sit next to her. Lance replied, "Just because I don't want to sit next to Harriet doesn't mean that it doesn't hurt to find out that she doesn't want to sit next to me."

Fawn Plush was of the opinion that turnabout is fair play. Lance felt that, though this might generally be the case, there are exceptions and this was, in his opinion, one of them. Fawn asked why this should be an exception, and Lance requested that Fawn "butt the hell out." Fawn took exception to this, and the Chair allowed the exception to be taken.

At this point, Harriet invoked the Golden Rule. The Chair ruled the Golden Rule out of order. Harriet objected, and the Chair overruled her objection.

David Alms queried the Chair as to what was the big problem, anyway, since both Harriet and Lionel seemed to be content with their new seating assignments, and nobody else had objected. The Chair replied that the big problem, anyway, was that this would set a dangerous precedent: acceding to a committee member's wishes just because nobody objected to it. He was sure that this would come back to haunt the committee, big time, in the future. In any case, Lance's action had been in contravention of his authority, as Chair, to determine the seating arrangement, and since the Chair had precious little authority, erosion of any portion of it was a matter of grave concern to him.

David suggested that, in the interest of moving forward, Harriet and Lionel should switch back to their originally assigned seats and just not look at one another. Harriet and Lionel agreed, and the meeting returned (actually, moved for the first time) to the topic at hand: the Firm party.

"Last year's party at the Moosetoe Lodge and Country Club cost the Firm over $40,000," reported the Chair. "We're under some pressure to cut the cost this year. I would welcome any ideas."

"Perhaps we should move the party from the Moosetoe," suggested Lionel.

"That's impossible," said the Chair.

"Why?"

"Because Stanley Fairweather is a founding Moosetoe."

"We could cut out the shrimp appetizers," suggested Lance. "That would save a pretty penny."

"Are you kidding?" asked Harriet. "People come to the party expressly for the shrimp appetizers. If we cut those out, we'd probably lose twenty-five percent of our attendance."

"Great," said Lance. "That would further reduce costs."

"We wouldn't have to tell people that there wasn't going to be any shrimp," suggested Lionel. "That way, we could cut costs without affecting the attendance."

"I don't think we could do that," countered Fawn. "The SEC would regard that as the omission of a material fact."

"I doubt that we're subject to SEC regulation in sending out an invitation to the Firm party," opined Lionel, sarcastically.

"I'm not so sure. We'd better have some research done," Fawn ventured.

"We could do away with those little hotdogs with barbeque sauce," suggested David. "They're not very good, and I always drip them on my pants. I've ruined six pair of pants on cocktail hotdogs, and I don't even like them."

"Let's not get bogged down in minutiae," cautioned the Chair. "Our function is not to decide the appetizer menu. That's what we have the Appetizer Subcommittee for."

"Maybe we should have a cash bar," suggested Lance. "We could even rake off a little profit for the Firm to offset the cost of the rest of the party."

"Yes, we could stand to cut down some on the drinking, anyway. I don't think it looks good to our summer associates to have partners staggering around the place. Didn't Rob Mentor go home with the wrong woman last year."

"He did, but that had nothing to do with the drinking."

"What do you mean, it had nothing to do with the drinking?"

"Well, Rob used to be married to her, and he just forgot. It was several spouses ago."

"I think we should have name tags this year," said Harriet. "It's no good pretending anymore that we're a small firm in which we all know one another. Especially since we invite spouses; nobody knows the spouses."

"That's not true," objected Lionel. "I know my spouse. True, I sometimes call her by our daughter's or my mother's name, but I definitely know her when I see her."

"Are we going to allow attorneys to bring significant others?" asked Lance.

"I suppose we should permit that option, but I'm still going to ask my wife," said the Chair.

"Why do we have to call them 'significant others'? What's wrong with 'date'?" asked Harriet.

"The word 'date' is offensive to certain spousal equivalents."

"Spousal equivalents? What the hell is that?" asked Lionel.

"It's somebody who talks like a spouse, walks like a spouse, but is really a duck," explained Harriet.

"Now you're pulling my leg."

"Gotta get up pretty early in the morning to put one over on you, Lionel."

"Shouldn't we at least have guidelines as to how significant the significant other has to be to qualify as significant? I mean, otherwise don't we run the risk of having just any old other at our party?" asked Lionel.

"What if we say, 'significant enough to be invited to the party'?" suggested the Chair.

"Good, at least that gives us a standard."

"Maybe we should do away with the spouses. I mean, not invite them to the Firm party. That would save a lot of money," offered Lance.

"Most of them probably don't enjoy the party in any case. They just come out of a sense of responsibility," said Harriet.

"C'mon, *nobody* enjoys the Firm party, you know that," said the Chair. "We all come out of a sense of responsibility. And if I've got to come, my wife is going to damn well have to come, too."

"Now wait a minute," said Lance. "If it's really true that nobody enjoys the Firm party, maybe we should just do away with it. That would make the Finance Committee very happy."

"As Chair of the Appetizer Subcommittee, I object. Doing away with the party would wipe us out, destroy our raison d'être," complained Lionel.

"Au contraire," said Lance. "Your subcommittee could decide what kind of appetizers you would have had, had there been a Firm party."

"But what about COUPLE?" moaned the Chair. "If there's no party, our whole committee might just as well be abolished."

"Not at all," offered Lance. "We will always have a function, and a very important one, at that. Every year, we will need to decide whether to reinstate the Firm party."

Whereupon, the committee voted unanimously to abolish the Firm party, "without prejudice to reinstatement."

Secure in Our Beliefs

To: All personages, legal and non-legal
From: Major Richard Hawkins, ROTC
Subject: Security

In the light of attacks by certain Forces of Evil (FOEs) who, for security reasons, will remain unnamed, the Firm has seen fit to revisit and revise the Firm's security procedures. I am proud to announce that the Executive Committee has appointed me, Major Richard Hawkins, ROTC, as your Chief Security Officer. In my opinion, they could not have chosen a more ideal personage to fill that important Firm role, given the distinguished service that your Chief Security Officer provided to a branch of the armed services of this fine nation only a decade or two ago, under the courageous and able command of our Firm's stellar Executive Director, Lt. Colonel Clinton Hargraves, CPA.

The Executive Committee has authorized the Chief Security Officer "to adopt appropriate rules, regulations, and procedures in order to safeguard the person, possessions, papers, files, data and other stuff of the Firm and its clients." In accordance with this authority, your Chief Security Officer has proposed, promulgated, and adopted the following provisions, which shall take effect right this second. These provisions are highly confidential and should be kept top secret at all costs. Remember: loose lips sink ships.

Protection of Chief Security Officer. As the continued security of the Firm is dependent upon the survival of the Chief Security Officer, the following shall apply:

a. The office of the Chief Security Officer shall be moved to an undisclosed location.

b. Two guards shall be assigned to patrol the area around the undisclosed location of the Chief Security Officer's office. The guards will be told that they are playing a war game in which they are protecting the Queen of Sweden.

c. Access to the office of the Chief Security Officer shall be afforded only to those with a "need to see." In this age of technology, nobody has a need to see.

d. Communication with the Chief Security Officer will be through the Firm's intranet, using a code that will be provided to the Firm's Security Committee. For security reasons, the membership of the Firm's Security Committee will remain a secret.

Protection of the Firm's Executive Committee

a. Because the Executive Committee is the Firm's brain trust, protection of their brains is of utmost importance to the Firm and its clients.

b. The Chief Security Officer having determined, after deliberation, that protection of the Executive Committee's brains without the protection of their entire bodies is impractical, the Firm has obtained bulletproof bubbles for each member of the Committee. It is anticipated that the bubbles will not materially affect communication with other Executive Committee members, since they did not communicate much without their bubbles.

Protection of the Firm's Other Partners, Associates, and Staff

a. Other partners will be equipped with combination beeper/monitors. These will allow the Chief

Security Officer to monitor partner whereabouts and warn them in the event of imminent danger.

b. Associates. The Chief Security Officer has instructed the Firm's staff to "kinda keep an eye out" for associates and to give him a buzz if it looks like they may be wiped out by FOEs.

c. Staff. The Chief Security Officer regrets that it is impossible to protect everyone. This should not be taken by staff as an indication that they are not valued by the Firm, as other things could be further from the truth.

Protection of the Firm's Offices

a. To protect our offices, the Firm will be hiring groups of Friskers, Spotters, and Thugs.

b. Friskers. The Firm is in the process of installing metal detectors that will be located between the elevator areas and the receptionists. All clients and guests will be screened, and Friskers will search client and guest carry-ins for staple removers and other weapons of destruction. As a precaution, the Friskers will do random strip searches of clients and guests. Regrettably, this procedure may result in delays of up to two hours at peak frisking times, but the Firm anticipates little opposition, since everyone is used to these delays at airports. To simulate an airport environment, the Firm is installing screens with client arrival and departure infor- mation. Firm personnel will be issued ID cards and secret words, which will change daily, to obviate the need for their screening and frisking. The first secret word is ... oops, almost made a big mistake.

c. Spotters. On each side of the Firm, we will be building booths for Spotters, who will scan the horizon with telescopes to identify aircraft that may be headed for the Firm's offices. In the event that a Spotter spots a suspicious plane, the Spotter will ring a bell and all Firm personnel will vacate the building via the stairs. The Firm anticipates a number of false alarms as we work the bugs out of this system, but such is the price of eternal vigilance. The false alarms will provide good exercise and should help reduce the flabbiness that Rocky, head of our workout facility, has noticed on many Firm personages.

d. Thugs. The Firm is seeking approximately fifty large, surly young men (prior criminal record desirable, but not essential) to patrol the hallways as a final line of defense for the Firm.

e. Friskers, Spotters, and Thugs will wear Fairweather National Guard uniforms, and will be armed.

Protection of Data and Files

a. All Firm computer files will be backed up hourly and taken to remote locations.

b. Our photocopy department has been instructed to make an extra copy of every document brought in for duplication, and these extra copies will be taken directly to offsite warehouse locations. The cost of the duplication and storage will be passed on, at a substantial profit to the Firm, to our clients, since we are only doing it for their benefit.

Though, as I have said, I believe that the Firm has an outstanding Chief Security Officer, no Chief Security Officer, however outstanding, can do the job alone. Security is, and must remain, everyone's business at Fairweather, Winters & Sommers. I am therefore designating each Firm personage a Junior Security Officer and charging you with the responsibility of remaining ever-alert to the threats of FOEs. The Forces of Evil are everywhere, believe me. (In fact, I think one may be looking at me right now.) We must protect one another's backs. Only through constant vigilance can we hope to make our Firm safe, secure, and relatively free from danger.

The Whole Lawyer

"What's that smell?" asked Seymour Plain. "Something must be on fire."

"No, nothing's on fire. It's just the incense," replied Percifal Snikkety.

"Incense? At the Firm?"

"Yes, I think the Firm's new Director of Spirituality is holding his first meeting in the main conference room. Why don't we go by and see what it's all about."

"I'm not so sure I *want* to see what it's all about."

"C'mon, Seymour, you've got to be more open minded than that. You've always struck me as a spiritual person."

"And you've always struck me as somebody who's going to get a sock in the schnaaz."

Seymour and Percifal walked into the main conference room, where a man with a beard, wearing only a dhoti and a turban, sat cross-legged atop a tray full of legal pads on the rosewood conference table, his eyes closed. Incense was burning at the four corners of the table and a prayer wheel stood behind the table. Chairs had been pushed back from around the table, and a group of approximately twenty lawyers, partners and associates were sitting on mats around the table, barefoot, cross-legged, and eyes closed.

"That guy looks vaguely familiar," whispered Percifal to Seymour.

"Yes, he does," replied Seymour.

"Ping, pinnngg, pinnngggg." The leader sounded chimes, and the group gradually opened their eyes and looked up at him.

"Salaam. Welcome, welcome home. I am so very pleased

to see so many of you here so early in the morning. We are going to embark together on a journey. Today we will be taking our first step together. But being lawyers, you will have noticed that I welcomed you home and said that we are taking a great journey together. How can we be home and on a journey at the same time? Paradoxically, home is the journey and the journey is home; they are one and the same. For it is said that a journey of a thousand miles must begin with a single step.

"Much of what I say may not make sense to you at first, but I ask that you trust, because trust is the road on which the journey is traveled. Without trust there is only cynicism, and cynicism is the roadblock that makes the journey of a thousand miles seem as if it were a journey of nine or ten thousand miles. For it is said that a picture is worth a thousand words, and if there are say ten thousand words to a mile, then ten pictures is one mile. And I won't even get into kilometers.

"You may ask me, 'Swami Fantu Ishram Dhin, tell us please who you are and how you came to be our leader.'

"Well, I say, fair enough. I was the child of well-to-do parents, Hyman and Sharon Kaplan, who named me Seamus Goldberg. I excelled in high school in darts and was awarded a darts scholarship to Dartmouth College, which was somewhat surprising, as darts was not then an intercollegiate sport in the Ivies (nor has it become one since). At Dartmouth I eschewed alcohol, forming instead a Dartmouth tea society, soon emerging as its chairman and sole member. Having no real interest other than avoiding the real world, it was only natural that I should sign up to take the LSATs, on which I scored in the 99th percentile, which gained me admittance to Harvard Law School.

"At Harvard, I performed well enough to land a job during my second summer with one of the several hundred prestigious law firms from around the country who suck up to Harvard law students each fall. As I refrained from exposing myself in the reception area during my 2L summer, I was offered a job on graduation, which I accepted, because you'd have to be crazy to turn down that kind of money."

"That's why he looks familiar," whispered Percifal to Seymour. "We hired this guy."

"As I began studying for the bar exam, a vision appeared to me of what the rest of my life would look like if I followed the course I was on. I would work exceedingly hard and succeed in finding ever narrower areas of expertise. My salary would increase, and my spending habits would follow suit, making it inconceivable for me to imagine scraping by on any less money than I was then making. If I was fortunate, I would succeed in becoming a partner in the law firm I joined, thus incurring even greater obligations, earning far more money, but still only barely enough to scrape by on. And when I made partnership, I could look forward to the next forty years of my life, which, if I were successful, would produce even greater income, a corner office, and a place on the Executive Committee.

"This vision produced such a powerful effect on me that I bolted out of the bar review course that very day, and escaped to India. There I encountered Swami Sri Paramha Ram Singh, who had had many deep mystical experiences before the age of 11, when he entered an ashram to perfect his inner vision. I was told that the Swami would lead me to that rare state of God-realization, oneness with God.

"I began to purify my body, my speech, and my mind. I woke up at 3:30 each morning to sing divine hymns, gurbani, and meditate, to enjoy the amritveta, the nectar hours, before sunrise. I sought awareness to give me direction. I sat in padirsasan position, like this."

"This is very uncomfortable," Seymour, who had assumed the position himself, blurted out, unintentionally.

"Change is always uncomfortable, sir. But for a solid year, I changed everything I could. I studied, I meditated, I breathed, I recited my mantra, I ate only vegetables, I gave up cigars, I squirted salt water up my nose and vomited to cleanse my body."

"And then what happened?" asked Seymour.

"On the anniversary of my joining the Swami, I decided to get the hell out of there. It dawned on me that pure truth was suffocating me. I needed to make truth matter, so I decided to come back and introduce some of those called to the bar to what I had learned, so that they could add meaning to their sorry lives.

"Now I would like to ask you to close your eyes again, and to follow me in guided meditation. Remember what I said earlier about trust.

"As you close your eyes, empty your mind of all thoughts. Breathe in, and now out, very slowly. Feel the air enter through your nostrils and pass through your body. Breathe deeply and evenly, relax your face and your body completely, and feel a gentle calm come over you.

"In front of you now is The Law in all its majesty. You may see it as a large purple mountain or as a still lake. You may see it rushing in like a wave breaking on the shore. Perhaps you see before you the scales of justice, balanced evenly in the hand of a blindfolded woman or the U.S. Supreme Court building with its sturdy columns.

"Absent from your vision are time sheets and clients bitching their heads off about paying the perfectly reasonable bill that you just sent to them. Absent, too, are committee meetings and law students waving flags of entitlement at you.

"You are practicing law the way that you once thought you would. You are finding intellectual challenge and ample, though not excessive, financial reward. You are working with colleagues who share your dedication to the practice and who are willing to pitch in to do whatever needs to be done for your clients, who are appreciative of all of the effort that you and your colleagues are putting forth. You are finding meaning and satisfaction in your work. You have awakened your inner lawyer, and the two of you are really happy campers.

"The thought has not even crossed your mind that you are blowing some perfectly good billable time by sitting here on the floor with your eyes closed and your legs crossed. You are not worried in the least that were many of your fellow partners and associates to come into this room, they would regard you all as major loons. These things do not worry you because you are in touch with your inner lawyer, let's call him or her Justice Truself. Justice Truself wears a long, black robe and a contented smile. 'Oyez, oyez, oyez,' the Justice calls to you. 'Oyez, oyez, oyez.'

"The journey that we have all embarked upon today is not an easy one. The siren call of Circe, the client, is loud, and the passage between the Scylla of the billable hour on the right and the Charybdis of the collected fee on the left, who would snatch you from the ship of meaning, is narrow and perilous. But we will navigate it together.

"In a moment you will emerge refreshed from this leg of our journey. My advice to you, frankly, is that you get back to work and not fritter away the whole damn day. Pingg, pinggg, pingggg."

"So what do you think, Seymour?" asked Percifal as they arose and left the room.

"I'd say the Swami was about half successful."

"What do you mean by that?"

"Justice Truself is happy as a clam, but I don't see a lot of difference in dear old Seymour Plain."

Partnership Assets

"Did you hear about Jim Freeport?" Executive Committee member Harry Punctillio asked his fellow EC member, Robert Mentor.

"No, what happened to Jim?"

"Nothing happened to Jim, it happened to us. He's leaving the Firm?"

"No kidding? Isn't he a bit young to be retiring?"

"He's not. He's joining Effete & Mighty."

"No. Jim never struck me as an Effete-type guy."

"Well, he's about to become one, Bob. And he's the fourth partner we've lost this year to one of our competitors."

"We've got to do something about this."

"Just what I was thinking."

"Good, we're in agreement then, Harry."

"The question, though, is what to do."

"Exactly, Harry, that is *precisely* the question. Why don't we talk about that sometime?"

"How about now?"

"Don't we need to get committee consensus on this, Harry?"

"We'll need committee consensus to take action, Bob, but we don't have to get committee consensus to talk. The partnership agreement provides specifically – and I think I quote here – 'that nothing herein to the contrary notwithstanding shall be construed to prevent partners from talking to one another outside of committee meetings, from time to time.'"

"By golly, you're right. I'd forgotten all about that provision. Good thing somebody thought to include it. So, then we're free to proceed."

"Sure are. What do you recommend?"

"Well, off the top of my head, I'd say the problem is one of loyalty. We've got to instill a greater sense of loyalty in our partners."

"And just how would you propose we do that?"

"I don't know, maybe an oath?"

"You think a loyalty oath would keep partners at the Firm?"

"Maybe not. But if they felt more a part of the Firm, in on decisions, you know, that might help. Perhaps we ought to go back to having weekly partnership meetings."

"Bob, we ditched those weekly meetings ten years ago because they were a waste of time. Now we can't even get partners to come to our annual meeting."

"You're right, that's probably not the answer. And I guess physical restraints wouldn't work, either. It's a damn shame to lose these good people, though, after all the Firm has invested in building them up. But everything seems to come down to the bottom line."

"Wait a minute, Bob, I think you've got something there."

"I do?"

"Yes, you do. What's the Firm's most valuable asset?"

"I don't know. I suppose our computer system cost quite a bit, didn't it? And the art collection wasn't exactly peanuts, either."

"No. I don't mean equipment, Bob. People. People are our most valuable asset, and partners are our most valuable people, isn't that right, Bob?"

"Can't quarrel with you there, Harry."

"So, that's it, isn't it, Bob?"

"Sure is, Harry. *What's* it?"

"If partners are valuable assets of the Firm, our most valuable assets, we've got to start treating them as such, right?"

"Couldn't agree with you more on that one, Harry."

"So, we wouldn't let our computer system, or our art collection, walk out the door without our getting compensated for them, would we?"

"No. I don't think our computer system or art collection could actually walk out the door, but I think I see what you're driving at. You think the Firm ought to get compensated when our partners leave."

"Gosh durned right I do."

"But the firms that are stealing our star partners are already paying top dollar for them, and our best partners are worth it, so I don't think we could get any more for them."

"That's just the point you were making."

"Yes. Ah, could you expand on my point a bit, just so I can make sure you've understood it fully."

"Of course. What you were saying, that is, if I comprehend you correctly, was that the problem was not so much that we were losing partners, but that we were losing the *wrong* partners, our best partners.

"That's exactly what I was saying."

"We've got plenty of partners who aren't producing. What we've got to do is figure out how to lose the partners we want to lose."

"But that won't be so easy to do, will it, Harry. After all, our competitors are going to want to nab our most productive partners, the way they always have in the past."

"Sure, but *we* know the value of our partners far better than the firms to which they're going. All we've got to do is tout the virtues of our deadwood partners and pawn them off on our competitors for big bucks."

"And how exactly will we benefit from this, Harry."

"Well, our underproductive partners know who they are. Most of them are concerned right now that we're going to bid them a not-so-fond sayonara. If we can tell them that we are going to unload them on other firms at a big premium, they'll be happy to give us a portion of that premium."

"That would only be fair."

"Fairness is all we're after. So, we'd be taking partners who were a net loss to our firm and creating a new stream of revenue from their sale. That revenue will make the Firm more profitable, which will mean that we can pay our productive partners more and thereby increase our chances of retaining them."

"But that's not the only advantage, Harry."

"It's not?"

"No, that's the brilliance of your idea. Having to pay all of that money for our unproductive partners is going to make our competitors a lot less profitable."

"So that means that *their* most productive partners are going to be on the market and will be ripe to be picked off by a firm that has trimmed its own fat."

"Exactly. And that lean and mean firm just might be Fairweather, Winters & Sommers."

"None other."

"But there's one problem with your idea, Harry."

"Clue me in."

"Well, we can't just go to another firm and offer our partners to them. They'd be very suspicious."

"You're right, that would never work."

"But that's the beauty of your idea, Harry: it creates yet another potential stream of revenue."

"You're right. Remind me how."

"Well, since we can't approach another firm directly to sell our partners, we do it the time-honored way: through a headhunter. But not just any headhunter. No, we wouldn't entrust our partners to just any headhunter. We create our own captive headhunting firm to peddle our underproductive partners at a premium, and then collect a headhunting fee on top of it."

"There's one big problem with all of this, though."

"What's that?"

"We'll never be able to explain this in a way that the EC could understand it."

You Can't Tell a Book Group By Its Cover

For many years, the discussion in the Fairweather, Winters & Sommers coffee room rued how lawyers at the Firm had once been interesting liberal arts majors, but had turned into dullards. Coffee room inhabitants wondered aloud whether they were still capable of discoursing on topics other than fees collected, hours billed, cases won or lost, deals closed or cratered, kitchens remodeled, cars purchased, and spouses divorced.

One day, Lydia Milife, a magna cum laude graduate in English from the University of Southwestern North Dakota, broached an idea to her brethren and sistren in the coffee room—why not start a book group? Of course, broaching the subject in that way produced responses that included the following: "it would take too much time," "time spent reading would not be billable," and "that's a dumb idea." Nonetheless, as Lydia's idea leaked outside the coffee room, she began to attract a following of lawyers who thought her idea was a gosh darn good one.

Within eight months, a group of lawyers began to meet informally to discuss the formation of the group and to flush out the issues that might arise. In only four more months, the group had decided to hire a professional book group leader to facilitate the discussions. Selection of the leader required another six months, as the spouses of the lawyers interested in the book group all belonged to book groups themselves and promoted their leaders for the new position. Eventually the group decided to hire Rachel Neuberg, an experienced facilitator, and actually met.

Not long thereafter, Rachel tendered her letter of resignation, and the group disbanded. What led to Rachel's departure is best captured in her letter to Lydia, which is set forth in full below.

Dear Lydia:

Thank you for the opportunity to serve as your book group discussion leader, however briefly. Unfortunately, for the reasons detailed below, I must resign.

As you know, we met at your house at 6:30 PM on May 15. The first half hour or so was consumed by many of your lawyers grilling me about my credentials. I did not mind this, as I wanted your group to be comfortable with me as your leader. The tone of that discussion might have been a tad less confrontational, but let's leave that be.

One of your lawyers raised the question of what the book group should be called. Frankly, none of the other groups that I have led in my twenty-six years as a facilitator has named its group, but then I guess I've never led a group of lawyers. I would have expected the naming to be a simple matter, that a name such as the Fairweather, Winters & Sommers Book Group would easily prevail. I had not anticipated that use of the Firm name could create legal concerns of the magnitude expressed by several lawyers. I was impressed with the scope and variety of names suggested, ranging from the Latin, Ex Libris, to the somewhat hipper Rappin' 'Bout Books. In the end, I suppose that The Book Group was probably a safe and reasonable choice.

We plunged next into a discussion of officers of The Book Group, an issue that again, foolishly perhaps, I had not anticipated would be so controversial. Belated, but sincere, congratulations on your selection as Chair, Lydia. I'm sure that this will add an impressive line to your already sparkling curriculum vitae.

Most groups I've led have a somewhat less formal means of adding members, but I suppose a three-quarters majority assures a certain desirable level of acceptance by other members of the group. (I think that you were wise to eschew developing a written test for admission to the group.) The provision for exclusion from membership by the same majority is unusual in my experience, as was the specification of possible grounds for expulsion. I wondered how one would establish "conduct deleterious to the reputation of the group or any of its members," but I did not feel it my place to raise this issue and did not want to further delay the meeting.

I did anticipate that we would discuss how often the book group would meet, but it did not occur to me that anyone would suggest biannually. Most of the groups with which I am involved are composed of more voracious readers than that. Settling on the 15th day of every other month, regardless of the day that date falls on, was a rather unusual resolution of the frequency issue, but I suppose it could work. I was sorry to have had to reject the suggestion of one member that the meetings be held at my house, but that is a service I simply do not provide.

Book groups often consider whether to serve food at their gatherings. Over the years I have heard the pros and cons, though not nearly so many pros or cons as I heard in your discussion. For example, it never occurred to me that one of the cons of serving food is possible liability of the group for food poisoning, nor did I suppose that the indemnification provisions relating to that liability could prove so knotty. Silly me. Though I realize that members of your group may have different tastes in food and dietary restrictions, it seemed like overkill to insist on setting in advance the menus for the first four sessions. I must admit that the suggestion made by one of your group to allocate the costs of the meals according to the number of pages of the assigned book read by each member, on the theory that those members who read the most would benefit the most from the session, was creative. At the same time, I cannot say that the counter argument presented, that allocating food costs based upon pages read would create a disincentive to complete readings, was without merit, either.

At last we got onto the topic of books, which I had rather thought would consume the entire evening. By this time, it was after 10 PM, and I expected that the blood sugar level would have dropped dramatically. If it had, you could not have proved it from the tenacity with which your group attacked the consideration of which books to read.

The first issue raised was how we would decide which books to read. In retrospect, I may have stepped beyond the bounds by suggesting that I would be happy to make the choices, as I do for other groups. Judging from the derision with which my suggestion was greeted, I must have. Still, I think it was unnecessary for members to respond with "over my dead body" and "you must be smoking something, Honey." I appreciated your intervention at this point, and the short break you called, during which I was able to regain my composure.

As you will recall, we had no shortage of suggestions for methods of choosing our books. I recall only a few, including:

> whatever's #4 on the NY Times bestseller list
> rotating the choice among group members
> taking whatever is being read by your spouses' book
> groups
> no Russian novels
> flipping a coin

We never resolved this issue, as the discussion was deflected to considering what types of books we would read. The early discussion on this topic revolved around non-substantive issues. Certain members favored hardback books because they were easier to read, while others leaned towards paperbacks because they were lighter, both in weight and on the pocketbook. Proponents of hardbacks pointed out that those concerned with cost could borrow the book from the library, or get them from a bookstore, read them carefully, and return them for a refund. There ensued a discussion of the morality of reading books and returning them to a bookstore. Several other members advocated limitations on the number of pages that a book chosen by the group could have. One group member who had a rather long commute to work proposed that only books available on tape be eligible for selection.

At this point somebody noted that there had been an assumption that the group was in accord as to what type of subject matter should be covered in the sessions. Upon exploration—big surprise—it was determined that not only was unanimity lacking, but a majority was lacking, as well. One member wanted to read law-related books, one classics, one poetry, one history, one humor, and one wanted to concentrate on how-to or self-improvement books (though he appeared to take umbrage at the suggestion by another member that his interest in self-improvement was certainly warranted). A suggestion that the group rotate the categories of books that it read was rejected by one member, who allowed that he would "rather die a slow, painful death than read poetry."

At this point, one member noted that the clock had struck the bewitching hour and suggested that the group had made excellent progress for one night and should adjourn to consider the remaining issues at another time. I informed the group that I would rather die a slow, painful death than attend another organizational meeting of The Book Group.

Just as hope had about been given up by all, a member suggested that the group read books that had been made into movies. In this way, members could limit their time commitments by spending only a couple hours at a flick. This suggestion seemed to be welcomed by all in attendance, and the meeting was adjourned.

So, in the end, it seems that The Book Group has become a movie group. Happily, that means that I am not the appropriate person to lead your discussions and so I hereby tender my resignation, effective immediately. I have decided not to bill you for the session I attended, since the thought of you debating how to allocate my bill is more than I can bear. I wish you the best of luck in your endeavors and will be most interested to learn what you decide to change the name of your group to. Might I suggest The Last Picture Show Group.

Sincerely,

Rachel Neuberg

Onward and Ever Upward

Traditionally, the firm of Fairweather, Winters & Sommers, like most large law firms, reviewed the performance of its associates periodically—and that was that. As associate turnover became a problem, though, somebody got the bright idea that partners might be part of the cause of that turnover, and that associates should review partners on the performance of their partnerly duties. In other words, instead of just downward evaluations, there should be upward evaluations, as well.

Now, when it came to partners reviewing associates, Fairweather partners had always been rather dismissive of associate concerns about the fairness of the review process. As the shoe switched feet, however, partners began to change their tunes as to how much process might do as due. Months of haggling led to adoption of a system that provided safeguards to protect partners who, it was feared, might otherwise be maligned by an upward evaluation. These safeguards included the right to counsel at Firm expense and a hearing before a panel of three retired judges of the state supreme court, sitting as FURP, the Fairweather Upward Review Panel. Below is the transcript of an oral argument made before the FURP by Adian Wynn, counsel for partner Godfrey Bleschieu.

"Good morning, Your Honors."

"It's 3 PM, Mr. Wynn."

"Thank you, Your Honor, I stand corrected. Good afternoon, Your Honors. May it please the FURP, I appear before you today to prevent grievous mischief. I have filed a motion to enjoin circulation of the upward evaluation forms."

"Wait a minute. You are before us and there has not even been an evaluation of your client, Mr. Bleschieu?"

"That is correct, Your FURPships."

"'Your Honors' will do, Mr. Wynn. What standing does Mr. Bleschieu have to complain? How has he been harmed? It may be that the upward evaluations of Mr. Bleschieu turn out to be highly favorable and that he is benefited by the process."

"That is certainly possible, Your Honors. Indeed, if this were a fair system, that would certainly be the result, as Mr. Bleschieu is a striking example of exactly what a partner should be."

"Well then, why don't we wait to see how the system operates?"

"Your Honor, we contend that the results could lead to irreparable harm to Mr. Bleschieu and that the upward evaluation system as established is fatally flawed and should be enjoined from operation."

"And just how is it fatally flawed?"

"In many ways, but to cite just one, it is not truly an upward evaluation system."

"Why not? Associates are evaluating partners, so surely that's upward."

"Yes, it is, but are first-year associates evaluating second-year associates? Are third-year associates evaluating fifth-year associates? Are junior partners evaluating senior partners? No, they are not."

"But, Mr. Wynn, the fact that the system may not be as fully upward as possible is surely not a reason to set it aside. What other flaws do you claim the system has?"

"Some partners have only very few associates working for them, so their evaluations will be based on very few opinions."

"But the same is true of associates who may work for very few partners. You are not suggesting to the FURP that associates who have not worked for a partner be asked to evaluate him, are you?"

"No, though I understand that was suggested by somebody during the debates on the provision, and that several partners thought it was a good idea. But how do we know that the associates who are turning in the evaluations are actually the ones who work for the partner?"

"We were told that each associate was assigned a code that had to accompany the submission of an evaluation."

"Yes, but there could be some shenanigans."

"Mr. Wynn, 'yes, but there could be some shenanigans' does not constitute a sufficient legal argument on which to throw out the upward evaluation system. Is that all of your arguments?"

"Not by a long shot, Your Honors. Here's another one for you. These evaluations are anonymous, which is unfair, unconstitutional, and un-American. Partner reviews of associates are not anonymous, and what's sauce for the goose should damn well be sauce for the gander."

"But in the case of partner reviews by associates, there's a concern that if their reviews were not anonymous, associates would not be candid for fear of retribution. Partners do not have a similar concern in evaluating associates."

"Ah, but now they do. The upward evaluation could be used by associates to tarnish the reputation of a partner in retribution for unfavorable performance reviews that those associates received from the partner. And the effect of that upward evaluation could be devastating. Mr. Bleschieu's compensation could be affected, or he might even be terminated, put out on the street with barely a shirt for his back."

"Come now, Mr. Wynn, aren't you being a bit unrealistic here? When's the last time anything bad happened to a partner for something he did to an associate?"

"With these upward evaluations, Your Honor, a new day is a-dawning.

"A new day may be a-dawning, Mr. Wynn, but not *that* new a day. And anyway, I thought the firm had taken care of the retribution problem by requiring that the upward and downward evaluations be done simultaneously."

"Yes, but once an evaluation gets out, it could circulate like wildfire, and Mr. Bleschieu's reputation could go up in flames. I know that you'll point out that the firm has hired an outside accounting firm to receive and tabulate the evaluations, but things could leak."

"Yes, of course, things *could* leak, and pigs could fly and a lot of other things could happen, Mr. Wynn, but it seems to me and, if I am reading my fellow justices correctly, to the full FURP that you have not shown any reason why we should jump in to throw the system out before we see how it operates. There's no reason to believe that the stellar reputation you say Mr. Bleschieu deserves won't be recognized fully in the evaluations."

"Well, actually there is, Your Honors. Unfortunately, we've heard some nasty rumors around that a couple of associates are going to slander Mr. Bleschieu in their upward evaluations by claiming that he is impossible to work for."

"And how do you come by this information, Mr. Wynn?"

"We have our sources."

"Mr. Wynn, I'm afraid that 'we have our sources' is not going to cut it. You're going to need to be a little more forthcoming than that with the FURP."

"Okay, we placed a small recording device in the sugar container in the associates' coffee room...."

"You've bugged the associates' coffee room?"

"I suppose you could say that."

"Well, what would you say?"

"I'd say, we've taken certain precautions."

"Okay, Mr. Wynn, what did your precautions reveal?"

"Well, we heard associates talking about how Mr. Bleschieu never gives them feedback, doesn't provide them the information they need to do what they are asked to do, and takes credit himself for all of their work."

"And is that true?"

"Well, there may be a kernel or two of truth."

"So then, why are you so intent on preventing associates from saying that?"

"Frankly, Your Honors, my client, Mr. Bleschieu, is embarrassed and wants to do better."

"Sounds to me like upward evaluations are working already."

And the FURP denied the requested injunction.

Kindly Refrain from Feeding the Attorneys

Though much of the proliferation of non-lawyer staff at Fairweather, Winters & Sommers has followed the path blazed by other firms, on occasion the Firm has ventured out in front of the pack. Nowhere has the Firm left the competition further behind than in its decision to hire Gunther Klaus, which attracted so much attention in the legal community that it netted a front-page article in a prominent magazine. The publisher of this book is indebted to *IGLOO, The International Gazette of Legal Organization Oddities*, for granting permission to reprint the following article in its entirety.

KLAUS TAMES FAIRWEATHER FIRM

"To be honest, I thought they were kidding," says Gunther Klaus of his first contact from the prestigious international law firm of Fairweather, Winters & Sommers. "But since the call came from Stanley J. Fairweather himself, I figured I would take him up on his offer of lunch, especially since I had never eaten at the Bigwig Club."

Klaus can be forgiven his skepticism about the call from Mr. Fairweather. A world-famous lion tamer for more than two decades, Mr. Klaus has spent the past eighteen years as Director of the Gotham City Zoo. While he has been highly sought after in many fields, the world of large law firms had not previously been prominent among them.

"I was impressed by Mr. Fairweather's sense of humor from the get-go," Gunther recalled in his interview with IGLOO. "Stanley had arrived early for lunch and was seated at a window table. As I approached and stuck out my hand to greet him, Mr. Fairweather sprang to his feet and lifted his chair, pointing its legs at me in a mock effort to fend me off. Damn spunky guy for an octogenarian.

"We had ourselves a chuckle or two, before settling in to talk business," Klaus recalled. "Mr. Fairweather explained why he had called. Apparently, some years ago, the firm had adopted a childcare policy in an attempt to attract and retain lawyers who were contemplating having a family. That policy had been a rousing success, but recently had come under strong attack from a coalition of lawyers who had elected not to have children, and from lawyers who were beyond the childbearing stage of life."

IGLOO confirmed in independent interviews with Fairweather lawyers that the childcare policy had become a source of friction around the Firm. Speaking on condition of anonymity, associate Frieda Brooks told IGLOO, "The world is overpopulated as it is, in a totally major way. Further procreation is irresponsible, so why should some of us be penalized for choosing not to have children, huh?"

Asked why she felt she was being "penalized" for not having children, Brooks explained, "The Firm has only so much money to spend on benefits, let's call it $H. If the Firm chooses to spend a certain amount on childcare, let's call it $R, then the Firm has only $H minus $R, or $J, to spend on its responsible, non-procreating lawyers, instead of the full $H. So, in that sense, childless attorneys are being penalized." Another Fairweather lawyer agreed strongly with Frieda Brooks, making his point this way, "I agree strongly with Frieda Brooks."

Klaus told IGLOO that Stanley Fairweather confided that, although the Executive Committee had initially been dumbfounded by the criticism leveled at the childcare policy, it had rebounded quickly and appointed an Ad Hoc Committee on

Childcare Policy Criticism [surprise, no acronym] to examine the problem. After hearings on the question, and considerable study, the ad hoc committee presented the EC with five alternatives:

1. revoke the Firm's childcare policy
2. grit your collective teeth and ride out the storm
3. denounce the opposition as "more than a little out of step with the times"
4. adopt a non-childcare policy that would pay every lawyer who did not have a child in the Firm's childcare program an amount equal to the average cost to the Firm for attorneys who have children in the program
5. none of the above

The Executive Committee elected #5, none of the above, concluding that the other alternatives would be either:

1. impractical,
2. ineffective,
3. counterproductive,
4. stupid, or
5. all of the above.

Stanley explained to Klaus that, left suddenly with no viable options, the Executive Committee was forced to don its thinking caps and notify the partners. (A provision of the Firm's partnership agreement required that the EC notify the rest of the partners whenever it donned its thinking caps, since that was generally acknowledged to be a dangerous time around the Firm.)

By this point, Klaus told IGLOO, he had counted the meeting a success. Asked how that could be so when he was still in the dark as to the reason he had been invited to the Bigwig, Klaus said that the tuna tartare was sufficiently outstanding that "nothing else really mattered much."

Eventually, Stanley explained to Gunther why he had been contacted. The Executive Committee had concluded that the real problem in the childcare controversy was that it was a discriminatory benefit. Some Fairweather attorneys were unable to have children, even if they chose to. To counterbalance this benefit, therefore, the Firm needed something that any attorney could avail himself of. Since any attorney could own a pet, and since many Fairweather attorneys loved their pets better than their children, in any case, the Firm decided to construct a pet care facility, and had concluded that there was nobody better to head up this effort than Gunther Klaus.

"Naturally, I was flattered," Klaus told IGLOO. "To be selected from all of the candidates worldwide to be Fairweather, Winters & Sommers' first Zookeeper was quite an honor. It presented new challenges for me, and when I heard what the salary would be, I simply could not turn the position down."

Klaus said that he was unprepared for the actual challenges that he encountered in his new position. "Naively, perhaps, I had not expected that the Firm would appoint COZI, the Committee on Zoological Issues, to work with me. At first I welcomed this participation, as it seemed to me a measure of the Firm's interest in the animal effort. The notion that COZI was something I should welcome passed quickly, however, in fact, at the first COZI meeting, when I was presented with a list entitled 'Preliminary Questions for the Zookeeper.'

"Though, mercifully, enough time has passed that I cannot recall all of the questions raised, mentioning a few may give you a sense of what was on COZI's mind. What types of animals would be permitted? Some favored any type of animal. Others suggested only invertebrates. Some were concerned that people might be afraid of certain animals. Others thought 'that's their problem, the scaredy cats.' Since some of the scaredy cats were clients, however, COZI adopted a list of permitted species.

"Another question was whether, since childcare was available only for sick and pre-school children, the Fairweather Zoological Gardens (as it had been named) would be available only to sick and especially young animals. The issue of whether animals could be kept in attorneys' offices proved to be highly

controversial, as was the question of whether Nails Nuttree's parrot, which swore a blue streak, would be allowed admittance. (The conclusion on the latter issue was that since Nails was not barred from the office because of his foul mouth, it would be unfair to exclude his parrot because of the bird's dirty beak.)

"Controversy also swirled around the issue of whether the animals would be housed in a central location, or scattered around the offices, perhaps with each floor housing a distinct species. Proponents of the latter approach argued that by putting a picture of the species behind the reception desk on each floor, employees and clients could more easily tell which floor they were on. Opponents, however, pooh-poohed this notion, saying that the Firm was 'not some damn parking garage.'

"Perhaps the hottest issue became whether to install a massive salt-water aquarium in the main reception area, a move favored by the Firm's scuba divers, who pictured themselves donning their scuba gear at lunchtime and diving in to feed the tank's residents. Ultimately, plans for the tank had to be scuttled because load limits of the building would have been exceeded by the weight of the tank."

Klaus reports to IGLOO that while not all of the kinks have yet been ironed out, he has now settled into his new job and has 'relatively few regrets.' Much of his time these days has been spent in meetings with the Firm's Finance Committee discussing how to convert the Zoological Gardens into a profit-making operation. The initial venture into that area has proved a big success. People seem to be more than willing to shell out the three bucks the Firm is charging for entrance to the Litigators' House, where patrons can watch Nails and his troops growl and devour their raw meat.

Which Solution?

By its charter, the Fairweather, Winters & Sommers Long-Range Planning Committee meets biannually to consider issues that are of "enormous importance to the Firm but of such sufficiently little likelihood of occurring that the Executive Committee is prepared to foist them off initially on the Long-Range Planning Committee." The topic on the agenda of the most recent meeting of the committee fit that definition to a T.

"I don't understand. What do they mean, we should consider 'this solution'? Which solution do they mean?" asked Sheldon Horvitz.

"Not 'this solution,' Sheldon," corrected committee Chair Herbert Gander, "*dis*solution."

"Oh, that's very different."

"But why would the Executive Committee be asking us to consider dissolving the Firm? Are things really that bad?" asked Hiram Miltoast.

"Who knows," said Herb. "After all, we're only partners, so why should they tell us?"

"I know that the Firm has been getting awfully large," said James Freeport. "That's caused a lot of problems."

"Yes, and quite a few lawyers have been leaving the Firm for greener pastures," added Helen Laser.

"Yes, and I suppose it's not exactly a good sign that becoming a residential real estate agent is now considered 'greener pastures,'" mused Hiram.

"No," agreed James. "And I think the rigors of managing an organization our size has gotten to some members of the EC, so that may be behind their request for us to consider dissolution, as well."

"In any case, though, ours is not to reason why," Herb reminded the committee, "so we'd better just get to business, before it's too late."

"What do you mean 'before it's too late'? Do you think somebody is about to dissolve us involuntarily?" asked Helen.

"No," replied Herb, "but it's 7:30 already, and you know that our committee bylaws require that we adjourn by 9:15, so that two of our members can catch the 9:35 train home."

"I recommend that we start by considering the question of under what circumstances the Firm should dissolve," suggested Sheldon. "To get the ball rolling, in my opinion we should dissolve only if things get really, really bad."

"Well, that's not too much help, Sheldon, is it! I mean, what does 'really, really bad' mean, anyway?" asked Hiram.

"I'd say that it means not just 'bad,' or even 'really bad,' on the one hand, but not 'really, really, really bad,' which is pretty darn serious, if you ask me, on the other."

"And how would we know whether things were sufficiently bad to dissolve, Sheldon?" asked Helen.

"Oh, *we* wouldn't have to know that," said Sheldon. "That would be up to the Executive Committee to determine."

"I see. So then what use would it be for us to tell the Executive Committee that they should dissolve the Firm if things got 'really, really, bad,' if it was up to them to make that determination, in any case?" queried James.

"Well, they have to have a standard for their decision, don't they?"

"Okay," said the Chair, "why don't we all adopt Sheldon's standard and move along with the rest of our work."

"Excellent," said Sheldon. "Now that's progress. As long as I'm on something of a roll here, I might tell you that I also have a suggestion as to how we should dissolve, in the event that the Executive Committee so determines."

"I have the feeling that we're going to hear your suggestion in any case, so why don't you let it fly, Sheldon."

"That would be my extreme pleasure, Helen. Though I'm going out on a little bit of a limb here, I'd say that we ought to dissolve very quickly and very, very carefully."

"And what led you to that conclusion, Sheldon?" asked Helen.

"Okay, try to follow my reasoning here. If we dissolve, then the Executive Committee, according to the recommendation we just made, is going to have to have determined that things are 'really, really bad,' right?"

"Right," answered the committee, more or less in unison.

"I thought so. Okay, if things are really, really bad (and we won't know this for a fact, only that the Executive Committee has determined that they are), it's going to be important that we neither dilly nor dally in executing the EC's orders. Lawyers might say that 'time is of the essence.'"

"Right, lawyers might," agreed the Chair.

"So we're going to act very quickly, I'd say."

"I hate to ask this, Sheldon, but why 'very quickly,'" asked Helen.

"An excellent question, Helen. In a situation that's 'really, really bad,' merely acting 'quickly' is not good enough because, as my dear old grandfather of blessed memory used to say, 'he who hesitates is lost.' On the other hand, though, to act 'very, very quickly' would not be wise, either, as 'haste makes waste.'"

"Did your dear old grandfather of blessed memory say that, too, Sheldon?"

"No, actually I think that's from *John Heywood's Proverbs*, first published in 1546. But getting now to the second part of my formulation, that it be done 'very, very carefully,' I think you can see why that would be necessary."

"Yes, I think we can," said the Chair, foreclosing further discussion. "But why don't we try to identify what steps we would have to take if the Firm were to dissolve."

"Good idea," opined James. "One thing we'd certainly need to do is inform our clients that the Firm was dissolving."

"Yes," agreed Helen. "They would need to know, right away. And we'd have to make sure that their matters were attended to in a way that didn't disadvantage them because of our dissolution."

"We'd certainly want to garner all of our assets," said the Chair.

"Or at least pull them all together," suggested Sheldon.

"Collecting all of our accounts receivable might be a problem," said Hiram. "People are not so quick to pay money to an entity that doesn't exist anymore."

"Yes, we might even need to hire a collection agency to go after what we're owed,' said James.

"That's awfully distasteful, isn't it?" said Sheldon.

"Maybe, but not half as distasteful as not collecting what we're owed," replied James.

"Besides our accounts receivable, we have an awful lot of personal property around the Firm that we'd need to liquidate," said Helen. "Everything from furniture, to paintings, to plants."

"I'd buy a couple of the plants," offered Sheldon, "if the price were right."

"Thanks a lot, Sheldon, that should help," said Hiram.

"Happy to do it. I like those palms in the reception area. What would you think I could snag those for?"

"Sheldon, I think it's premature to be picking out particular plants," said the Chair.

"Probably so, but I just thought I ought to get my dibs in."

"A good deal of what we have would not be worth anything. For example, all of the things with our Firm name on it, like the stationery, forms, etc.," said James.

"Not everything with our name on it would be worthless," said Sheldon.

"Such as what?" asked Helen.

"Well, you know those nice brass letters that spell out our Firm name in the reception areas on each floor?"

"Yes, what about them, Sheldon?"

"I was just figuring here, on this sheet of paper, that if we could find a firm named Masters, Hart & Winer, we could sell them those letters and still have 2Es and an F, M, R, S and W left over."

"Good work, Sheldon. Why don't you keep on figuring other firm names," suggested the Chair.

"Be my pleasure."

"We'd need to calculate how to divvy up our liabilities," pointed out Hiram. "There are some pretty big ones, too, like the 20-year lease we signed. We'd need to sort through how the partnership agreement allocates those."

"And don't forget that we'd need to provide for the payment of retirement benefits to our older partners," added Helen.

"Don't our obligations to pay those benefits end on dissolution?" asked the Chair.

"I guess we'd have to look at what the partnership agreement provides on that, too. And if it's ambiguous, as most provisions of our partnership agreement are, we could wind up in some serious litigation over that one," said James.

"Worfiter, Shaw, Siemmer & Tranes, and it comes out exactly even," announced Sheldon.

"Thanks, Sheldon," said the Chair. "Y'know, given all of the difficulties of dissolution, I think we need to revise our earlier decision."

"What do you mean, Herb?"

"I think 'really, really bad' is too lax a standard. We ought to dissolve only if the Firm is 'totally in the tank.'"

And the Long-Range Planning Committee voted (Sheldon dissenting, in favor of his 'really, really bad' standard) to submit the 'totally in the tank' standard to the Executive Committee, where it languishes to this day, unconsidered.

The Last Word

In our attempts to wine and dine law students for the privilege of overpaying them, and in our efforts to make associates happy, even in our focus on the business of the Firm, we too often ignore the core of our Firm – the partners. After all, without them we'd have no Firm.

What it means to be a partner at a large law firm today differs a whole lot from what it meant in the not too distant past. I used to know my partners. Time was, in fact, that I knew my associates. Hell, I even used to know the people who worked at our firm and who had the dumb luck not to be lawyers.

Now I've got people I call partners who I couldn't pick out of a police line-up. Many of them I've never broken bread with. Some of them I've never met, and a few of them don't even speak my language (I mean, literally don't speak my language; over the years, quite a few of my partners have not spoken my language in the colloquial meaning of that phrase.) And many of the people I call my partners may be here today and gone the next, as soon as a more attractive offer comes along.

How do you create a real law firm under those circumstances? That's one pretty damn good question.

Stanley J. Fairweather

End of an Era

The large law firm world lost one of its true giants yesterday when Stanley J. Fairweather, founder, managing partner and guiding spirit of Fairweather, Winters & Sommers, passed his last non-billable hour on this earth.

Born in Chicago in 1918, Mr. Fairweather attended the University of Chicago (BA, magna cum laude, 1940) and the Harvard Law School (LLB, magna cum laude, 1943). He served with distinction in the U.S. Army, entering as a lieutenant in 1943 and leaving as a colonel in 1945.

While Mr. Fairweather was active in many civic and charitable activities, his true love was the law firm that he founded in 1952 with Oscar E. Winters, P.C., James Q. Sommers, P.C., and the late Fairbut W. Cooler (who died before P.C.s were invented). Mr. Fairweather shunned becoming a professional corporation himself, often quipping to those who asked, "I've never been P.C. in anything, and I'm sure as hell not about to start now in order to avoid a little bit of liability."

Members of his firm were devastated at the news of Mr. Fairweather's death. Reached at his office, Oscar Winters said, "We shall not see Stanley's like pass this way again. We are converting his corner office into a permanent shrine." An obviously choked-up Fairweather litigation head, Nails Nuttree, blurted out, between sobs, "It was my extreme privilege to work in Mr. Fairweather's long shadow and to watch him pirouette gracefully through life. He was a veritable colossus striding among us pygmies."

Mr. Fairweather directed that his remains be cremated and housed in a vase on the main reception desk of the Firm.

As he finished dictating the above obituary, Stanley turned to his secretary, Bertha, and added, "Now if either Oscar or Nails bites the dust before me, you'll need to remind me to put those quotes into somebody else's mouths. I rather hope that old Nails sticks around, though. I'd love to see him try to deny to the press that he said what I quoted him as saying. And I'd give anything to see his face when he discovers that he's not moving into my corner office. That's it for tonight, Bertha. Have a good weekend. See you Monday."